ROSS PEROT

ROSS PEROT
The Man Behind the Myth

KEN GROSS

Random House   New York

Grateful acknowledgment is made to William Morrow & Company,
Inc., for permission to both directly quote and closely paraphrase
excerpts from *On the Wings of Eagles* by Ken Follett. Copyright © 1983
by Ken Follett. Reprinted by permission of William Morrow &
Company, Inc.

All photographs are from the private collection of the Perot family,
except that of Ross Perot with Prince Charles, which is by David Woo,
Dallas Morning News.

Library of Congress Cataloging-in-Publication Data

Gross, Ken
   Ross Perot : the man behind the myth / Ken Gross.
      p.   cm.
   ISBN 0-679-74417-7
   1. Perot, H. Ross, 1930–   . 2. Presidential candidates—United
States—Biography.   3. Businessmen—United States—Biography.
I. Title.
E840.8.P427G76   1992
973.928′092—dc20   92-18602
   [B]

Manufactured in the United States of America
9 8 7 6 5 4 3 2
First Edition

For Andy

Foreword

Upon hearing I was writing the foreword of this biography, an acquaintance asked, "Why would someone like you choose to get messed up in politics?" Meaning that "nice" people should not risk getting their hands and souls dirty in the political sink. Well I happen to think that "nice" people should be right in the thick of the work and risk the consequences.

It is not a matter of choice, anyhow. All of us have always been involved in politics—from the day of our birth; we are part of the human community—part of the *polis*—We, the people—that's us—*all* of us.

Furthermore, from age twenty-one we have all held important political office—the most important office of all: citizens in a democracy. It's a job for life, just like being a judge on the Supreme Court. The only matter in question is what shall the record of our individual terms of office be? We don't need any more passengers or spectators—those jobs are filled.

Whatever I may think or say or believe or hope— the crux of the political matter is what will I *do*— what will I *work* for? When I come to the end of my term of office, will my answer to that tough question be an honorable one? Can I, as a Citizen, stand on *my* record?

The most pressing matter before the Citizens of this country now is the election of a president on November 3. If you haven't already gone to work for a candidate, it's about time you did. Who will it be?

What once seemed a foregone conclusion may now be an open question, in large measure because of the unexpected and unique entrance of one man into the presidential arena: Ross Perot.

Who is this man?

I'll tell you what I know. In 1958 I was a very junior employee in the Dallas office of IBM. The most talked-about man in that office was Ross Perot. He came to work earlier, stayed later, worked harder and smarter than anybody else. He attended the daily needs of his clients with care. At the same time, he had a long view of the impact computer technology would make on business and every other phase of American life. He was quickly known for his imaginative solutions to complicated problems.

I remember these things because he was held up to me as a model—a man to watch and emulate.

Over the years I've kept up with Ross Perot. It's not hard because his accomplishments often have been newsworthy, and his success has been the stuff of which legends are made. That he is now a serious candidate for president of the United States comes as no surprise.

As with every other candidate, I don't agree with everything he stands for and don't support everything he's done. He is not the Messiah. But I do say Ross Perot deserves to be taken seriously—to have his qualifications considered carefully. I'm especially interested in the private life of Ross Perot. What about his roots—his family values—his marriage? What about his education—what kind of student was he? Who are his friends—and who are his enemies? What's his religion? How has he handled failure and adversity? What life events have shaped Ross Perot in such a way that he thinks he could handle the monumental task of being president?

The dramatic entrance of Ross Perot onto the main stage of American political life has radically affected the sense of what's possible on November 3. If he has aroused your interest, and you share my questions, then you will find this book a useful and fascinating look at the man behind the myth.

—Robert Fulghum
June 1992

Prologue

On Thursday, February 20, 1992, Tom Luce, a high-powered corporate lawyer, was on a treadmill in the bedroom of his plush North Dallas home, trying to put some mileage between himself and middle age, when he heard a familiar East Texas twang coming out of the television set. It was the gnarly voice of his boss, Ross Perot, the impatient billionaire, who was a guest on the popular Larry King talk show.

Luce, longtime counsel to the swashbuckling and wildly unpredictable Perot, was amused, but not particularly surprised, to find Ross turn up electronically in his bedroom. The self-made and self-assured Perot had lately sought opportunities to point out the misguided ways of the world, and Larry King had a large audience for this sort of folksy gospel. And now that he'd sold off his interest in the computer company that made him the richest Texan alive—in 1984, General Motors bought Electronic Data Systems (EDS), a deal that ultimately earned him over $1.7 billion—Perot was a little antsy.

True, he was not completely idle. He still had his charitable foundations (which had given away more than $100 million to a variety of social causes) and a start-up corporate group that was developing a commercial airport and spreading homes and offices throughout the greater Dallas area. But Perot could not be content with merely keeping five or six projects in motion, like some circus juggler balancing plates at the end of a batch of sticks. Ross Perot was a daredevil. And he required pulse-pounding action.

At Christmas 1969, for instance, he leased two jets, loaded them with food, gifts, and reporters and tried to land in Hanoi to comfort American POWs. Though the North Vietnamese deflected the attempt, it called world attention to the plight of the prisoners, who later reported that their treatment improved after Perot's gallant gesture.

Then, a decade later, Perot became an international legend when he engineered the heart-stopping rescue of two of his EDS employees from an Iranian prison; a similar feat was later bungled by the Carter administration when it tried to free the sixty-one U.S. embassy hostages. (The Pentagon brought in Perot for "consultations" about that later mission, but he walked out in disgust when the planners got bogged down over the exact number of Iranians they could "afford" to kill during such a mission.)

Now Ross might be counted a cowboy fool by some or a loose cannon by others, but he had won a place in the hearts of Americans by his plucky can-do spirit and don't-give-a-damn candor. Folks didn't even hold it against him that he had $3.5 billion in the bank. Most people seemed to regard him as one of their own, albeit the luckiest lottery winner of them all. Which is not far off Perot's own self-estimation.

"I can show you a hundred people who work with me who are smarter than I am," he argues. "Heck, I wasn't even a smart student in school. Half the people I went to school with are smarter than me. Doctors. Teachers. Engineers. I just got lucky."

Whatever Perot's talents, he inspired boundless loyalty among his key staff by a thousand little thoughtful acts. Tom Luce did not just work with Ross Perot, he *admired* him and counted a lot of debts on the unpaid side of the ledger between them. Once, when Luce was appointed to the board of directors of his old school, Southern Methodist University, which had been rocked by a football recruiting scandal, Ross Perot donated $1 million to ease the possible financial consequences of the ensuing National Collegiate Athletic Association suspension. The money was given in Luce's name, and Perot did it quietly, without fanfare, without even mentioning it to his old friend.

But, though Ross Perot tethered his staff to him with chains of generosity, it was not always easy to work for a man who did not let his right-hand man know what his left-hand global strategy was doing. So, though seeing his boss on national television might not have been a shock, Tom Luce wished Perot had mentioned the upcoming appearance. There were times Luce trembled just picking up a newspaper, afraid to see Perot's latest exploit in tabloid lights. And today, as he slogged along on his treadmill, Tom Luce automatically picked up the pace a little. It was a common thing among all the corporate soldiers employed by Perot; they marched a little straighter and a little quicker in the presence of the old man.

The sixty-one-year-old Ross was in fine voice that night, plunking out his usual tune, denouncing the enfeebled incumbent political hacks and shortsighted business barons who had left the nation awash in a suffocating national debt and adrift without a moral or economic compass. Luce knew the melody by heart as Ross attacked the entire blind, leaderless mess. But suddenly, seemingly out of nowhere, Larry King interjected an unexpected question: "By the way, is there any scenario in which you would run for president?"

"Number one, I don't want to," said Perot.

But King, a determined seducer, sensed something soft and willing behind Perot's modest hesitation. He persisted. "I know, but is there a scenario?"

"Number two, you know, nobody's been luckier than I have. And number three, I've got all these everyday folks that make the world go round writing me in longhand . . ."

You could almost hear a drumroll building in the background as Luce marched faster.

". . . Now that touches me," said Perot, speaking of the letters and calls from a frustrated and bewildered citizenry. "But I don't want to fail them. That would be the only thing that would interest me. And so I would simply say to them and to all these folks who are constantly calling and writing, if you feel so strongly about this, number one, I will not run as either a Democrat or a Republican, because I will not sell out to anybody but to the American people. And I will sell out to them."

King lunged ahead: "So you'd run as an independent?"

Perot almost ignored him, speaking over his head to the viewing audience: "Number two, if you're that serious—you the people are that serious—you register me in fifty states, and if you're willing to organize and do that . . ."

"Wait a minute. Are you saying? Wait a minute. . . ."

Perot was saying something indelible, something that took away even the unflappable King's breath. The veteran host was trying to nail it down, applying all his journalistic skills, but the moment was too rich. Presidential races don't get launched on talk shows, except by zany, maverick, wildcatting Texas billionaires who play only by their own idiosyncratic set of rules.

"Hold it! Hold it! Hold it! Hold it! Hold it!" hollered King, unable to hold it.

"Well, wait a minute. Are you saying groups all across America—all across America—can now, in New York, Illinois, California, start forming independent groups to get you on the ballot?"

A done deal. And Perot, who has a reputation for shooting from the hip, but who, in fact, never moves without having a pretty good idea where he will land, spoke again: "Now then, God bless you all who have written me and called me. The shoe is on the other foot."

That's when Tom Luce lost *his* footing and nearly fell off the treadmill. He shouted out to his wife, Pam, that old Ross had done it again. They were no longer on a treadmill. They were running for the White House.

The next few weeks were a blur of activity and speculation as citizen committees—gently nudged by Luce and other Perot hands—sprang up from coast to coast and as far out into the Pacific as Guam. Perot announced that if he was placed on the ballot in all fifty states (a condition he would later modify to meet technical obstacles), he would devote whatever money it took—some have estimated $100 million—to the election campaign. He would not accept any government matching funds, once again tapping into the electorate's revulsion for political corruption.

Pollsters went daffy as this new ingredient blew open their careful calculations. Overnight, George Bush slipped even further in the national esteem, and Bill Clinton suffered anew as a vast constituency of undecideds and halfhearted voters shifted to this late, uncommitted, but solid entry. The ears of the nation perked up at the clarion call of a man who didn't sound squeamish about getting tough, and, more to the point, had no incentive to lie. After all, Ross Perot didn't need the job; he had his fortune. He did not enjoy the wounding game of jousting with the press; he wanted to keep details of his private life just that—private—and he couldn't understand why the media was demanding a line-by-line recital of his positions and beliefs, spelled out in contractual detail.

Perot said he'd come up with programs, but they would take time. He said his record of good works and charity, along with his roots in the solid soil of Texas folk wisdom, spoke more eloquently than any cheap sound bite. And, while his wife and family were by his side, he would do nothing to force them up front into the furious glare of his spotlight.

So many editorialists and political columnists dismissed him as a one-day wonder. But when his popularity didn't fade in the sunshine of the spring, they said that, in the end, Perot would simply take away strength from the Republicans, or from the Democrats, or maybe just possibly from both—a spoiler, at best. The "experts" still failed to take him very seriously. Yet the citizenry did; there emerged a volunteer army whose members ranged across the political spectrum, from alienated liberals to disappointed conservatives, who moved into the boiler rooms of his campaign committees from Maine to Hawaii.

Meanwhile, Ross Perot kept popping up on national television in his homespun way, and each time he was interrogated, or interviewed, he climbed higher in the polls. And though he continued to duck questions about his platform and his personal life, it was apparent that Ross Perot, candidate, was for real.

By the time the primaries concluded in early June, George Bush's and Bill Clinton's vote tallies seemed irrelevant; it barely mattered who voted for them, but rather who *wanted* to vote for Perot. Could Ross Perot win? became a very serious question, one that led to a critical corrolary: Just who is Ross Perot anyway?

ROSS PEROT

1

"I was born rich. Not in tangible things, but rich in the parents I had."

—ROSS PEROT

Ross Perot was born on the hottest day ever recorded in the East Texas town of Texarkana. The thermometer read 117 degrees on June 27, 1930. At least, that's the way it's recorded in the archives of the family legend. How else could they explain the iron will and tensile strength of Ross Perot unless he had emerged from a blast furnace?

It was an odd time and odd place to grow up. During the 1930s, Texarkana was split down the middle over the issue of Prohibition. Literally. The border between dry Texas and wet Arkansas ran right through the center of town. On one side of the main street, you could buy hard liquor, and on the other you could obtain undistilled gospel. The cultures broke along roughly the same lines. There was a standoff between the freewheeling cowboys and the tightly bound farmers. The cowboys favored the rowdy sections of town, where they could find bawdy houses with painted women and howl into the night. The farmers and merchants lived in quiet neighborhoods with well-attended churches and modest homes in which no meal was ever served without an accompanying taste of the Bible.

Inevitably, life in Texarkana was etched in sharp contrasts, but then, considering the nature of the people who lived there, the town was a small miracle of coexistence. During the nineteenth century, the delta of Bowie County had been settled by Scotch-Irish immigrants. They were bitter wanderers who had been uprooted from their native Scotland and replanted first in Ireland to act as a buffer between the Irish Catholics and the English landlords. But they were too proud to serve as the king's pike, and soon waves of immigrants flooded America and tried to take root in the fertile valleys of the East. Although the soil in Virginia and Georgia and Alabama was rich, the ruling class remained hard, and many farms soon fell to unpaid mortgage claims.

The immigrants who couldn't meet the ruinous

terms of their loans lost their acreage and home-
steads to the unforgiving banks. They packed up,
and the wagon trains moved on to the frontiers of
Texas, where the playing field was a flat landscape
that ran on forever. This wasn't the untamed Wild
West beyond the Pecos; it was nearer to the ship-
ping lanes of the great navigable rivers and the cotton centers where land was of a comprehensible size
and the farms were on a familiar scale. These were
self-sufficient individualists who didn't trust governments or strangers and ran their lives the way
they ran their businesses—with narrow margins and
adversarial assumptions.

But there was a softening influence, and it came
up from the lush bayous of Mississippi and Louisi-
ana. French-speaking traders introduced an engag-
ing merchant style into that cool and somewhat
mutinous society. They set up trading posts along
the Red River and swapped stories over backyard
fences and cracker barrels and sold bolts of cloth to
the farmers' wives while they were at it. Having a
joke and a smile in your kit was good business.

In the nineteenth century, Ross Perot's great-
grandfather, weary no doubt of the ordeal of the
relentless road, opened a general store in New Boston, Texas, twenty miles west of Texarkana. His son,

Ross's grandfather, Gabriel Elias Perot, took over the same shop and expanded the business to include cotton trading. The business flourished, although it was seasonal and required that a man offer additional merchandising features to fill in during the fallow periods. Breaking horses appealed to the romantic streak in the Perot line, and so they all learned to ride rough.

But each fall, when the crops came in, the farmers would bring their 500-pound bales of cotton to town, and the Perot Merchants and Wholesalers became the middlemen in a demanding and often thankless art. The seeds that would make Ross Perot a merchant prince were planted in those shrewd transactions. He would combine the hard, practical eye of his Scotch-Irish mother, Lulu May, with the sentimental charm of his paternal French ancestry to make an unprecedented business success. It was his grandfather and father who passed along the gift of the middleman—the ability to look at both sides of a transaction and locate the crack of profit. A middleman had to see the exact azimuth of value in things, and he had to be able to judge his customers with a dead-on certainty. There was no room for error. And since the farmers were suspicious by nature and the mill owners thrifty and tough by habit, it took a keen eye and the nerve of a burglar to come out ahead. And it took something else: charm.

Somehow, if you were going to survive in that business, you had to assemble transactions without making one side or the other mad that you earned a profit without the visible sweat of labor.

Calluses may have been few, but the deals were rarely clear-cut or easy. There was the element of risk. The traders had to buy the bales of cotton and speculate on the price they could get from the mill owners or from the foreign mills. They'd go in debt to the banks until the full circle of the deal came around and they realized a profit. A man *had* to be a speculator—willing to see the wildcatting possibilities in such an enterprise. A man also gained confidence in his judgment when he managed to stay afloat.

Among all the qualities that contributed to his success, Ross Perot's father was famous for his charm. He regularly drew a circle of listeners around him when he went to the barbershop on a Saturday afternoon. He had a natural gift for seeing the humorous side of life. "He reminded folks of Will Rogers," recalls his son. "Same kind of dry wit."

There was one signature story about Gabriel Ross

Perot that made him a kind of local legend. It also tells a lot about the prevailing insubordinate frame of mind when it came to "highfalutin'" public officials. It began one Saturday when the boys were sitting around the barbershop, shooting the breeze. The subject turned to politicians. That brought out some mischief in the senior Perot, who had a populist disdain for the pomp and rooster style that seemed to go with men in high office. He said that he didn't think it took much to get elected.

One of his cronies, disagreeing strongly, said that getting elected was a lot harder than it looked. G. R. Perot shook his head, and what's more, bragged that he could prove his point. He said that if he had a mind to, he could get someone elected to the Arkansas state legislature.

Naturally, that caused a few guffaws from the skeptics. Well, there was only one way to settle such a dispute. The friend offered to wager good money that Perot could not manage to get just anyone elected to state office.

Anyone, boasted Perot.

The friend stuck to a contrary view, and the consensus was with him. You could not just pluck someone off the street and ram him into the state legislature, no matter how puny the general run of legislators.

Yessir, said Perot—and you can even name the candidate, he added for good measure.

"So my dad's friend picked a crazy man," recalled the son recently. "He named Sniffer Arnold. Called him Sniffer because he sniffed snuff."

A bet was a bet, and Perot had to stand by his word that he could elect anyone named by the friend to the legislature. So he launched a campaign.

"My dad took Sniffer down, he bought him a new suit, got him a string tie, took him all over the district, campaigning," recalled the son. "My dad told me later, he said, 'Son, the day I knew we were going to win, we were driving down this little country road in an open car. Sniffer Arnold was sitting in the back waving. And as they drove by, someone said, 'Who's that?' And the other fella said, 'Man, that's the president.' At that point, I knew he was going to win."

After Sniffer had been elected an honorable member of the legislative body, he made a long inaugural speech in the well of the Arkansas legislature praising Gabriel Ross Perot, a man who had the vision to place him in high public office.

*   *   *

G. R. Perot was not the sort of person who would be crushed under the burdens of life. It was supposed to be tasted and felt and enjoyed, and he imparted this sensuous appreciation of life to everyone with whom he came into contact. He came by his benign world-view and his easygoing nature in spite of the hardships thrown against him. In 1913, at the tender age of fourteen, he had to drop out of school when his father died. He became a cowboy, not being able to manage the complexities of a business at that age. At the end of World War I, he moved from New Boston, Texas, to what was then considered a big, thriving metropolis: Texarkana. Texarkana had a population of about twenty-five thousand, and it had become a railroad hub because of the vibrant cotton trade.

Ross senior could see possibilities where others couldn't, and he went back into the cotton wholesaling business and did well. Folks liked Gabriel Ross Perot. He set up shop at 110 North Lelia Street, under a sign that read: G.R. PEROT COTTON BUYER; SELL IT. YOU CAN'T EAT IT. It was a modest start, not really much of an office. But it was enough, because Ross senior spent most of his time with the farmers anyway; he was the sort of man who didn't put much value in a lot of show.

Not all his time was spent in gossip or toil. There was a rich social life for the virtuous young businessman in Texarkana. There were church socials and picnics and Saturday night dances. For a big man, with what used to be called a generous figure, he loved to dance. And he was graceful and light on his feet. One night at one of the weekly dances, he met a slight young woman who was a shade over five feet and danced like a feather in his arms. Lulu May Ray had fair coloring, and there was a glint of something firm and knowing in her blue eyes. She was a high school graduate and worked as a secretary for a lumber company, and Gabriel Ross Perot could tell she was full of common sense, without an ounce of false pride or airs. From the moment they met and danced together, they sensed something sympathetic and durable about each other. A regard for intelligence and education. A wry sense of humor. Respect for old virtues and family. It was no surprise when they wed on February 25, 1923. He was twenty-three and she was twenty-five.

The first thing that he did was borrow four thousand dollars from the bank to build a redbrick bungalow at 2901 Olive Street where they would raise their family. It was painful to violate the vows of thrift, but Perot had no choice. He wanted a home with a big front porch where neighbors could visit and the family could sit out at night. In any case, he paid the loan back in full in a year.

Lulu May gave birth to their first child within a year of the marriage. It was a difficult birth. "The doctors said she shouldn't have any more children because it was too dangerous, so naturally, she went ahead and had two more children," recalled Bette, the first of the two beneficiaries of her mother's defiance. "She knew that there was a risk involved, but she was not going to be deprived of a family because of that."

On June 24, 1927, the firstborn, Gabriel Ross Perot, Jr., died of spinal meningitis at eighteen months of age. His death was, by all accounts, shattering for his father and mother. "It's not possible for parents to experience the death of a child and not feel it deeply," says Bette. Maybe, she thinks, it deepened her parents' appreciation for the rest of the family. And certainly what she can attest to firsthand is the devotion between her parents in the aftermath of the tragedy.

"They were very affectionate," recalls Bette. She remembers her parents holding hands and getting dressed up on Saturday nights and going to dances at the Club Lido nightclub. As a child, she'd watch them as they primped in front of the mirrors, and she felt the great satisfaction of a child who knows that her parents are in love. "That was great," she says.

And then, on that brutally hot day in June with only an electric fan in the doctor's office to provide a breath of air, came the birth of the third child. "That's my brother," said the precocious Bette when she was taken to visit her sibling, sixteen months her junior. He was born Henry Ray Perot, but later, at his father's request to keep the family name alive, he legally changed his name to Henry Ross Perot.

2

"There was a tough optimism around everybody we knew as children. I vividly remember as a child seeing the Red River come over its banks and wash away houses, barns, crops, everything. And the men just standing there like pieces of rock. Every now and then you'd see children crying and you'd see a wife with a tear in her eye—maybe. But no whining. The water'd go down, you'd rebuild it and hope it'd be a few years before it happened again. There's just some things you had to endure. That's just part of life."

—ROSS PEROT

There were hard lessons to be learned, growing up on the Texas side of Texarkana. Young Ross Perot learned that rivers overflowed their banks, and that without flood control or government help, you had to help yourself. That was the only way that things got done: Everybody "pitched in."

He also learned that other kinds of banks go bust, and that economies spin out of control and grown men can wind up hungry and alone. He saw it with his own eyes—muddy streets and an army of broken men. They'd approach the back door of the house on Olive Street in the evening, looking for help. The family would be out on the big porch, nodding up and down in the rocking chairs, and there would be a polite knock on the screen door. The men would hold their hats in their hands and offer to work in exchange for a plate of food. "They were really dirty and tough-looking," Ross once told an interviewer. "But my mother would feed them. People showed up every day, and she never turned anybody away. One day a man came by and said, 'Lady, do a lot of people come through here looking for food?' And she said, 'Yes.' And he said, 'Don't you know why?' And she said, 'No,' and he said, 'You're a mark.'

"He showed her where the tramps had made a mark on the curb in front of our house. That was a sign to other tramps that they would be fed there. After the man left, I said, 'Mother, do you want me to wipe that off?' And she said, 'No, leave it there. Those people are just like you and me. The difference is, they're down on their luck.'"

Lulu May seldom said no. No matter how thin their own menu—and there were times when she had to stretch the stock—she could always put together a plate of beans and some biscuits and gravy for the men who hopped off the freight cars with their bellies scraping against their ribs. Because of the big cotton crops, Texarkana was a railroad hub during the Depression; half a dozen lines crossed in East Texas. The hoboes rode the rails, and though some towns had laws against vagrants or brusque signs intended to shoo them away like pesky insects, Texarkana had an egalitarian pride—born, no doubt, out of the settlers' own experiences as unwanted homeless wanderers—and the rootless men who passed through were always apt to find a meal.

The people who came to the Perots' back door were not criminals. They were just hungry.

There were lifelong lessons imparted in a thousand spoken and unspoken ways, and young Ross Perot was a sponge, absorbing everything that his father said as they talked—man-to-man—when they were out riding in the evening. He pledged to his father that he would remain sober and swore he would not smoke or drink. Their home was a little more than a mile from downtown Texarkana, but it was beyond the blacktop, and there was an empty field across the unpaved road where they kept a couple of horses. Because the cotton business was seasonal, Ross senior was often able to spend a lot of time with his family. He came home for lunch every day, and there was hardly a dinner when he wasn't planted at the head of the table.

"My dad was my closest friend and he gave me a lot of time," says Ross. "We'd go to cattle auctions together. At first, he'd let me buy and sell saddles and bridles. And then I could buy and sell animals. But I couldn't take anything home. If you took something home, you had to feed it or care for it.

"I was what they called a day trader. You'd buy it in the morning and sell it in the afternoon and make a few dollars' profit if you were lucky. That taught me the art of trading and negotiating."

That, and watching every move his father made. There is a yellowing newspaper picture still floating in the family collection, of four men posing with the first bale of cotton ginned in Texarkana in 1947. Two of the men are farmers who raised the cotton, the third is the buyer, and the fourth is the broker, G. Ross Perot. This part of the deal was done on a handshake; for the broker to get the needed capital, a little more was required.

G. Ross Perot had to prove to the bank that he had a commitment from the farmer by bringing in a wagon wheel—a recognized token of a deal. Perot would stuff the wheel in the backseat of his 1929 Dodge (for which he paid cash) and deliver it to the loan officer; it was as good as the farmer's signature. Faith, Ross junior saw, was the key—that and how his father consistently treated the farmers fairly so they would always come to him first to buy their cotton.

In the dead of winter, they'd ride out into the country and sit over coffee or a soft drink with the lonely farmers, and in those quiet, fallow seasons, Perot saw his father sow the seeds of good business as well as friendship—and also civic duty.

"People who worked for him, when they got too old to work, he'd still take care of them," Perot remembers today. Not that he had any obligation. But, he said, they had to live, too. He felt an obligation.

"Every Sunday after church, he would take me down to the poorest section of town—the black section of town—and visit with these people. Just for one simple reason. He loved them. They were his friends. And white people didn't do that."

An ambitious boy had a lot of opportunities in a town like Texarkana. Some noticed his grit early, when he was eight and breaking horses. He'd get up on the horse and get thrown and break his nose, but he'd never cry. Not Ross. He'd bleed but not utter a sound. Just got right back on the horse. Sometimes he broke the horse and sometimes he broke his bones, but he didn't quit. This would become an epigramatic text for his view of life: "You need a guy on your team who's tough; when his nose is wrapped around his ear, he doesn't fold up on you."

He called it "getting knocked out" when he was thrown. Busted noses and concussions came with the territory. But then he figured a way to get the job done without getting a concussion. Using rags, he tied one of the horse's front legs. The horse, which has an inborn fear of falling, was quickly tamed, trying to maintain its balance. In five minutes, the horse would be exhausted. Soon, Ross became "a dollar horseman," so-called because he earned a dollar for each horse he broke.

Along the way he turned into a pretty good horseman and performed trick riding and fancy roping in local rodeo shows.

He also sold Christmas cards, garden seeds in spring, *Saturday Evening Post* subscriptions year-round, and he collected bad debts for newspaper classified ads. That was a tough job, but Ross Perot was all gristle. He learned about human nature and how to get past a bolted door.

"That was part of my business training," he says. "The most interesting thing to me—when I go back to Texarkana—is to reflect on how far I used to ride on a bicycle to collect a dollar and a half. That's what a classified ad cost for three days. They didn't pay for the ad because they didn't sell the item, typically. They didn't have much money. If you came to their door and told them you were here to collect it, most of them would pay. Because it was a debt that they had taken on."

Another job gave him an advanced degree in human nature, as well as sensitivity. At the age of twelve, he took on a paper route for the *Texarkana Gazette*, only he did it in typical Perot style. During the 1940s, the price of a subscription was 25 cents a week. The paperboy kept 7.5 cents. You had to work hard to earn five dollars a week on a good route. Times were still hard in 1944 when Ross applied for a route. He was competing against grown men who had to support a family, so there was no route available. As he explained to the *Dallas City* magazine, he opened new territory. "Texarkana had two slums," he told the reporter. "We didn't call them that, but that's what they were. New Town was the black slum, and Avondale was the white slum. They were next to each other. I told the men at the paper that I would start a route in New Town and Avondale if they would let me keep 17.5 cents of each subscription and give the paper 7.5 cents."

They laughed, as Ross recalls. They didn't think people in New Town or Avondale could read. But Ross thought otherwise. "They were the poorest blacks and the poorest whites in Texarkana," he said recently. "It was sandy streets, not even gravel streets, you couldn't ride a bicycle. And I rode my horse. It was a long route, and I went from door to door. And these people who were making nine dollars a week were really enthusiastic about getting the paper. And they paid me meticulously. They knew how important it was to get the paper. They knew how important it was to collect your pay. I had no trouble collecting."

If some people couldn't read, they used the paper as insulation. Perot was making twenty-five to thirty dollars a week, and his earnings spawned some resentment. It would not be the last time his gumption got on somebody's nerves. The circulation manager tried to change Ross's rate to what the others were getting. "I appealed directly to the publisher, Mr. C. E. Palmer," Perot has related. " 'Sir,' I said, 'I made a deal, and these guys are reneging.' "

Struck by the boy's courage, the publisher laughed and stuck to the original arrangement, which convinced Perot that whenever he had a problem, he should go directly to the top person, "the one who can say yes or no and get things done."

There are stories, still undenied, which claim that Perot also delivered newspapers to some of the bawdy houses on the wilder side of town. There are stories that he spent every Sunday morning outrunning would-be bandits.

"These were people who lost their money gambling and were trying to bring home a few dollars," he recalls. "They tried to grab the reins, but I never got touched.

"The general feeling was that it was unsafe to be there," he continues. "Nobody ever bothered me. I was down there at three-thirty and four in the morning in the very poorest part of town, and nobody gave me any trouble. There is a poignant memory I have about that time. In 1944, when I was fourteen, my dad had to have a kidney operation in New Orleans. Nobody was willing to deliver the papers there when I was gone because of the fear factor. So I told all my customers that I had to go with my dad, but I'd be back in a few days, and I hoped they'd keep taking the paper after I returned. I didn't expect them to want the papers that they'd miss when I was gone.

"And they said, 'Just keep the old papers and deliver them all at once.' I'll never forget that. I said, 'Well, you don't want old papers.' They said, 'That's not the point, son. If your dad's being operated on, you'll need the money.'

"Now these were people who were too poor to do anything for anybody else. And yet that was a society that worked."

3

"Ross, you ask me about Ross as a child. It's hard to remember incidents—actual incidents—because I was the older sister, and he was there, you know, but I was preoccupied. He didn't seem all that special. Not right away. Not at first. He was just my younger brother. It wasn't until later—a few incidents—when he began to amaze me."

—BETTE PEROT

A young girl growing up in East Texas during the ebb of the Depression had other things on her mind than a kid brother. There were dances and socials and sleep-overs. And, of course, the matter of simply growing up. The daily ordeal of figuring out strategies to handle adults, to say nothing of boys, overshadowed the presence of the little pest at the same breakfast table and lunch table and dinner table.

There were the usual sibling and family problems —spilled milk and secret candy bars and broken rules. Nothing serious, though, because the one thing the two Perot children agreed on was that they didn't want to disappoint their parents.

"We never got spanked," recalls Bette. "That was not the way things were done in our home. And there was none of that 'wait till your father gets home.' Our mother was not that kind of woman. If she had something to say, she said it. She said it plain, and she made her feelings clear. There was the look and the lecture. And that was enough. That was plenty.

"One time we were getting ready to go someplace in the car, and Ross and I got out there first. She was still getting ready. We were in the backseat, which is where we usually were when she drove, and there was a metal bar back there in the '29 Dodge, and somehow, we pulled it down. Broke it off. Now, maybe I did it or maybe it was Ross, but one of us said, 'Well, we shouldn't mention it. She might not notice.' Some chance. You couldn't slip anything past my mama. She came out to the car and saw it right away, and we got the look and lecture, and we did not go anyplace that day."

In the Perot household, there was an unspoken regard for the dignity and feelings of children. If Ross broke a rule, he would not be punished or even admonished publicly. Instead, the family tactic was to deal with the infraction privately, to prevent the humiliation of the child. "They would take him inside a room and close the door, so that in many cases I did not even know what he did," recalls his sister, Bette.

If there was one other solid point upon which both father and mother agreed it was on the value of education—Gabriel Ross, because he had to leave school so young owing to his father's death, and Lulu May because her own high school diploma gave her a solid sense of autonomy and self-worth.

And so when Bette was ready, the Perots sent her to a local private school, the Patty Hill School, which was an experimental grammar school. "It was in an old run-down two-story house," recalled Ross, who joined his sister a year later at the school. "The tuition was seven dollars a month for each child, and believe me, that was a sacrifice. The classes were very small. The lessons hard. But the foundation that we got . . ."

He shakes his head in wonder. True, the teachers used a ruler upon the knuckles of a fractious child. But there were daily Bible verses and extravagantly produced student plays, and art classes and literature classes, and the children had to answer roll call with a memorized verse—and in the end, the school left the children with high expectations. It also produced a crop of high achievers. "In Texarkana, in the middle of nowhere, we all knew Latin," says Ross.

The school was a marvel, and it led to long speculation on the part of H. Ross Perot about why there, on the lip of Texas and Arkansas, bloomed a renaissance of intellectual enlightenment. Part of the explanation, ironically, was the brute fact of the Depression. Highly cultivated, highly educated people—for the sake of security—would accept a modest role in the world, such as a grammar-school teaching position. It was a common enough phenomenon. Great artists went to work for the WPA, writers, too. This unexpected enrichment of the culture through governmental intervention revealed itself to Ross in another odd way. During the 1940s, a federal prison opened in Texarkana.

"A number of people on the staff moved down from Fort Leavenworth Prison," recalled Ross, "and their sons became my good friends. Every one of those people associated with the prison system was a college graduate. Two of my close boyhood friends' fathers worked in the prison system, and they were beautifully educated men, and their mothers were college graduates."

It left a strong impression upon Perot—conceptually and practically. Some of the well-educated federal employees took jobs in the public school system, and soon the quality of all education in East Texas rose like the banks of the Red River at flood.

"We [Bette and he] shifted over to the public schools after a few years," he recalls. "But we had the foundation. Now, there was another thing. It didn't matter what they taught you at school. My mother would see that we learned it when we got home whether they taught us or not. So this was a backstop. I learned in Sunday school and I learned in private school and I learned in public school and I learned at home. And all this learning was about values. I got vaccinated over and over again with values."

For Bette, childhood was simple and idyllic. The weeks had a soothing and predictable routine. On Friday nights, kids went to a movie. In her memory, *Casablanca* spins an endlessly romantic legend. (For Ross, a completely different and more practical myth shone from the silver screen. He was enthralled by a film biography of Thomas A. Edison,

Young Tom Edison. For years he dreamed of becoming an inventor, and his barn is today crowded with gadgets he invented—automatic watering troughs, automatic feeders for the stock, protected water lines so that you don't have to break the ice to haul water.)

If Friday nights were for movies, Saturdays were for dancing. The kids went to a gym and the parents to a nightclub. The songs of that time were pure sentiment, and left a residue of hazy, mellow recollections. Because of the railroad connections, performers like Cab Calloway stopped for a gig in Texarkana and played on the street called State Line, which divided the town between Texas and Arkansas. Ross's mother taught him to dance, and he remembers gliding across the bedroom floor with Lulu May in his arms and his grandmother Ray sitting on the sofa. "Her hands were never idle," he says. "She was either making clothes or hooking a rug or crocheting something. If she wasn't doing that, she'd be shelling peas. When I saw *Places in the Heart* [a film that depicts the hardships of independent Southern cotton farmers], I was looking at my childhood."

After the Saturday dances came the Sabbath. "My parents were both religious, though neither wore it on their lapel. But they practiced it. And we were in church every Sunday—it wasn't an option." On Sunday, after attending services at the Methodist church (a denomination Perot still belongs to), the family invariably sat down to a big dinner. Fried chicken. Mashed potatoes. Biscuits. And the sweet savoring of the week. Then everyone adjourned to the oversized porch and collapsed, letting the fresh air wash over them.

"We couldn't afford many things," recalls Ross. "But once a year we'd go to the New Boston Fair, which was twenty miles away. And once a year we'd also go to Ringling Brothers Circus in Dallas. Then, when I got a little older—and this is something I'll never forget, because this was a huge sacrifice on my dad's part—we would take the train to Fort Worth, go to the Fort Worth Rodeo, walk around the livestock show grounds, then catch the late train home because we couldn't afford to stay over."

One event still shines out from his youth: the 1936 Texas State Centennial Fair in Dallas. "I remember all the cars," he says. "At the age of six, my biggest dream was maybe someday I would own one." This from a man who became one of General Motors' principal stockholders.

A farfetched dream that grew on the plains of Texas never seemed completely out of reach. After all, Perot's parents told their children again and again that there was nothing they couldn't do. It was the Texas catechism: This country is so big and so rich that a person can latch on to a star and ride to the sky. Anything is possible. Anything at all, Ross was told. And the examples were not remote or hard to find. There was Uncle Henry, Lulu May's brother. Henry Ray decided that he was going to be a barnstorming pilot; the trouble was, he had no airplane. So he built himself one. He got some plans from a book and some wood from the lumberyard, and he sewed on his own cloth and painted it himself. He found a surplus old World War I Victory engine, fitted it into the frame he had fashioned, and in the end had himself an airplane. One that worked.

The example of Henry Ray's airplane was embedded in the consciousness of Ross Perot. He was convinced that a determined person could overcome any obstacle. And Uncle Henry carried his dream even further.

"There was nobody around Texarkana who knew how to fly, so he taught himself," recalls Ross. "He read about it. He studied it. And the first time he ever left the ground, he was by himself."

Henry Ray was like a character out of an adventure novel. He joined the service in World War II in spite of his advanced age—late thirties—and spent four years living off the land in China and Burma. He was an enlisted man working in the Signal Corps. A hero. And, like all romantic heroes, too modest to "brag on himself."

World War II became very personal with the Perot household. Ross had a cousin, Ross Hoffman, who was a bomber pilot in England, flying dangerous daylight missions over Germany. In all, there were three members of the family in the war. And up and down every street, citizens of Texarkana hung stars in their windows to indicate the family had a soldier off fighting against the Axis. Every now and then, someone in the neighborhood would be killed in combat, and that cold reality ran like a shiver through town.

There were other reminders that it was not a distant, far-off, bloodless war. Two defense plants sprang up during the war. The biggest was the Red River Ammunition Factory, and the second was the Lone Star Ordnance Plant.

"We were absolutely convinced that the Germans

would bomb us any night," Perot explains. "We had air-raid drills, we had blackouts, we had rationing. We collected scrap iron. We collected tinfoil as Boy Scouts. We collected books for the armed forces as Boy Scouts. I was buried in all kinds of projects like that. But we were focused on the fear that we were a target."

It did not occur to anyone to calculate the logistical improbability of such an attack. Why would the Germans mount such an effort—cross an ocean and break through the air defenses—merely to decimate a war plant in Texas? How could they manage it?

It didn't matter. Amazing things were everyday wonders. Jimmy Doolittle bombed Tokyo from a mythical base called Shangri-La. Soldiers leaped from planes and captured enemy strongholds. Anything was possible, and so they blacked out their windows and listened to the radio, and young Ross was held spellbound by the sound of Winston Churchill's voice. When Franklin Delano Roosevelt gave his fireside talks, the family circled the radio and listened with reverence.

There were certain rituals, certain emblematic tokens of the time, that endure. Ross's mother put a Norman Rockwell calendar in his room showing a

Boy Scout at prayer. (It is no accident that Perot collects Norman Rockwell originals now.) She worked with Cub Scouts and Boy Scouts, and Ross joined Boy Scout Troop Number 18 when he became twelve in 1942. He became an Eagle Scout in October, sixteen months later.

Even then, in his teens, he was a convincing salesman. His resourcefulness and imagination were impressive. When he had to compete against a talented athlete in tennis, he practiced in secret until he was good enough to win.

When it came time for Bette to go to college, Lulu May went back to work as a secretary to pay for her tuition. Bette was not going to be deprived of a college education. Ross had his heart set on the Naval Academy at Annapolis (an institution that had the added advantage of being free of charge), but his applications went unanswered. Instead, he attended a junior college in Texarkana.

"That was the first time I noticed he was different," recalls Bette. "There was a debate about moving the junior college off the campus of the high school. The sentiment at the time was to keep it at the high school, which was familiar. But Ross was against that. He saw ahead and argued that the college would not grow if it remained attached to the high school campus."

It was Perot, the student-body president at Texarkana Junior College, who first went to the chamber of commerce and explained how the students felt. His impertinence was not well received. Students simply didn't come brazenly forth like that. There was a professor at the school who told Ross not to give up. "Probably with his job at risk, he told me, 'No, you should say what you believe and stand on principle,'" Perot recalls.

Refusing to give up, Perot made another date to fight for the larger campus. He would again confront the city fathers on the issue of moving the campus.

"He marshaled his arguments, and he organized a campaign, and I had never imagined that he was so impressive," recalls Bette. "The only thing that my parents demanded—and we had a family meeting over the dinner table about it—was that he be respectful. No matter what arguments or what facts he brought to bear, he had to show respect to the school officials. And, of course, he did. He called them 'sir' and 'ma'am'—and he won his argument."

The Texarkana Junior College now sits on a

ninety-acre campus, and several thousand students attend.

This was, however, not the battle Ross Perot most wanted to win. He wanted to enter Annapolis. Josh Morriss, Jr., an older friend, was a midshipman, and when he came home in his uniform and spoke glowingly of the U.S. Naval Academy, Perot was even more determined to be admitted. He wrote letter after letter to his congressmen, but got no reply.

Finally, in 1949, fortune intervened. W. Lee "Pappy" O'Daniel was retiring from the Senate, and as he was cleaning out his office, he asked one of his assistants if there was any unfinished business. Just this one unfilled appointment to the Naval Academy, replied the aide.

"Does anybody want it?" asked the senator.

"Well, we've got this kid from Texarkana who's been trying for years," said the aide.

"Give it to him," said the senator, who never mentioned, or even knew, the name of Ross Perot.

"I wanted to be a cowboy. I wanted to be an inventor. I wanted to be a fireman. I wanted to be a lawyer. I wanted to be a federal judge. I wanted to be a doctor. But my big dream was always to go to the Naval Academy. Of course, we didn't have any political contacts."

—ROSS PEROT

He was a vagrant soul who spent the summer roofing barns around Texarkana with his father, then used the last two weeks of his vacation to hitchhike around the country. Somewhere. Anywhere. His curiosity was insatiable. "I wanted to see what there was to see," he says of this wanderlust.

His last great odyssey before serious schooling took him on a shoestring to Mexico. He had a few dollars in his pocket, and he went across the border, saw the sights, had a great time, then turned around and came back. He had $1.20 left to get home. "I hitchhiked night and day and finally got to a little town named Pittsburg, Texas, and they dropped me off there. And right across the street was an all-you-can-eat café for sixty-five cents. Well, I got my sixty-five cents' worth. I ate for a while. I never enjoyed a meal more in my life. I came home with fifty-five cents in my pocket."

Then he flew to Washington, D.C. The flight took eight hours, and there were numerous landings. From Washington, he boarded a bus that took him to the United States Naval Academy at Annapolis, Maryland. He watched the neo-Georgian buildings loom up on the horizon from the window of his bus, and he knew that he was at the end of one journey and the start of another.

As with many other important events in his life, Ross Perot took the oath as a midshipman on his birthday, June 27, 1949. He was a pint-sized midshipman, somewhere between five foot six and five-seven, but no one took much notice of his size. When he stood ramrod straight, with his hair at full attention in the military bristle cut that was to become a lifelong trademark, and looked you directly in the eye, it added some measure to his stature.

The academy was a revelation. He was surrounded by men from all the forty-eight states and candidates from Europe and from Central and South America. The routine was the usual brutal test of character—hazing, quick marching, long memorizations, hard study, strict obedience to random and arbitrary authority—and he thrived. "We didn't get out the first year," he recalls. "Everybody's always wondered if I didn't feel confined. And I laughed. I said no, there was more to do inside the gates of the Naval Academy than there was in Texarkana."

The exposure, the excitement, the competition converged to Perot's benefit. What began to emerge was an ability to make men listen, pay attention. It was an important trait—one called leadership. That first year when the leadership grades were posted, Perot was stunned to find himself at the top of the class. The rankings were made by classmates, upperclassmen, academic officers, as well as the military officers from the navy and the Marine Corps. He had no idea that he possessed this strange talent. "It was like learning you could play the piano by ear, literally. I looked at that and I said, Well, that's interesting."

They were ranked two or three times a year, and in almost every instance Perot came out at the top. In his sophomore year, he was picked as vice president of the class, and in his junior and senior years he was class president. He was also chairman of the Honor Committee his senior year, and it was during that tenure that a stubborn, uncompromising side of his nature publicly appeared.

"I seemed to have this pattern in my life of every now and then getting locked on an issue that gets kind of personal," Perot admits. "I was, at the time, in charge of the Honor Committee. We had one person that the midshipmen had found guilty of an honor violation. But because of who he was and who his parents were, everybody wanted to sweep it under the rug. So, on principle, I resigned from the Honor Committee and resigned as class president."

It was the only honorable thing he could do. But it didn't end there. Admiral C. Turner Joy, fresh from attempting to negotiate a truce in the Korean War, was superintendent of the Naval Academy at the time. He summoned Perot into his office. After the case was explained, he grinned at the young midshipman.

"He said, 'You know, you did the right thing.' And I said, 'Well, you-all have been teaching me for four years to stand on principle.'"

Admiral Joy was impressed and acted on Perot's principles. He punished the offending midshipman, and he convinced the upright Perot to take back his positions on the Honor Committee and as class president.

The reports about this bold, stouthearted, and plucky middie were not confined to the shores of Annapolis. During Perot's senior year they reached twenty-five miles into Maryland, where an eighteen-year-old junior from Pennsylvania—an American aristocrat whose father could trace his ancestry back to William Penn—was attending Goucher College. Margot Birmingham's forebears had regarded themselves first and foremost as patriots. One, a Quaker named Benjamin Fell, was a source of great family pride. According to the approved genealogy, Benjamin Fell was in the leather-goods business and supplied shoes for George Washington's soldiers at Valley Forge. The British placed a fifteen-hundred-pound bounty on his head. In spite of the reward and the scowls of his peers, who regarded any contribution to war as anathema, Fell stayed behind the lines with George Washington and did his part in the American Revolution.

After the war, though, Fell was shunned and had to leave Philadelphia. He moved to western Pennsylvania, where he established his own church. It is called the Old Fell Church, and the town is now called Washington, Pennsylvania. On Fell's gravestone, it says, "A friend of his country, a friend of George Washington and a friend of God."

Long afterward, Fell's distant descendant and Margot's father, Donald Cameron Williams Birmingham, became a banker and a lifelong Republican. He was a family man, and after his first wife (not Margot's mother) died, he remarried and raised five daughters. Margot remembers her childhood in much the same glowing manner as Ross Perot recalls his. "We were happy," she says. "My father was a good man, an honest man, and that is the way I will always remember him, as the strong soul of rectitude. For example we were once at a store buying food, and I took an ice-cream cone. Not a big thing. Nothing expensive. But each thought the other had paid and in the confusion no one paid; when it was discovered, he drove back— some distance—in order to pay for the cone. I know how it sounds, but it is a true story."

Margot was one of many young women attending Goucher College in the early fifties who drifted into teaching after majoring in sociology and anthropology. It was the custom for proper young women of that period to attend weekend functions at the Naval Academy, all under strict chaperone. "Many of the girls stayed with older women," Margot reminisces. "They were widows and they had homes close to the Naval Academy yard, and girls would spend the night there. Some of them would go weekend after weekend if they were seeing somebody regularly. And so these women who owned the houses became close friends to the girls and the boys who would come over."

One of Margot's friends was dating a middie who was a friend of Ross Perot's, and for a while there was a campaign to match up the two. "I kind of resisted this blind date for a long time, but I finally did go. My friend said that the reason you should go is because they're away for a football game and you don't have to go until late Saturday—you can just go out with him that one evening, to a dance. You can leave the next morning if you want to. So that's why I agreed to go."

It was October 18, 1952—the date is written in stone in her memory. She and her friend waited for Ross Perot in a restaurant in Annapolis. She sat there, and as everyone came in, she asked, "Is that Ross? Is that Ross?"

So great was his reputation that she expected John Wayne to crash through the door.

"Finally, he came in," she recalls. They spent the evening together and after dinner attended a dance at Bancroft Hall. There, surrounded by portraits of all the naval heroes from Farragut to Dewey, they danced away their qualms.

"It was love at first sight; it still is," recalls Ross Perot. "Every time I lay eyes on her."

Ross tells a story about that first date and Margot's ambivalence. According to him, she went back to Goucher, and her friends asked her to describe this mythic creature who was president of his class and chairman of the Honor Committee and had stood up to admirals. She was supposed to have said simply, "Well, he was clean."

Margot denies it. Although she doesn't remember the exact words, she says that her description of Ross was that he was "clean-cut." "You know, those boys are so scrubbed!"

If Ross fell for Margot at first sight, hers was a more complex, qualified reaction. "I knew that I wanted to be around him," she says. "Life was exciting when he was there. I remember thinking during one of those first weekends, I wonder what it would be like to live on a ranch in Texas? He was the first Texan I ever met. But at the same time I was afraid of being swallowed up by another strong man, like my father. He was smart enough to recognize that. He left for a year on a cruise while I was still in Goucher."

Before he left on his cruise, Perot graduated from Annapolis. Bette and her parents drove up from Texarkana in their 1949 Plymouth and were introduced to Margot. "We were worried that she wouldn't like us," recalls Bette. "Maybe we weren't fine enough. But the minute we met her, we saw that she fit right in. There were dinners and dances, and we were all glad that she had a chance to meet Dad, because he died two years later."

There were four destroyers making a round-the-world cruise that summer of 1953. Ross reported aboard the U.S.S. *Sigourney* on June 27, 1953—his birthday. At two o'clock in the morning, they upped anchor and left on a nine-month cruise that took them to twenty-two countries across seventeen oceans and seas.

"It never occurred to me that you could be in all four seasons in one day," Perot recalls. "See, we were down on the equator when the seasons changed. So we backtracked, circled, and did all four seasons in one day just for the heck of it."

The Korean War was still technically on at the

time, and Perot was the ship's chaplain (the boat didn't have a full-time cleric), among his other duties.

He was also damage-control officer. "From Norfolk, Virginia, to Midway Island, I could teach the dumbest guy in the navy how to do heart surgery. They'd learn how to perform first aid, how to keep the hatches closed. 'Cause we were going into combat. And I preached to standing-room-only audiences on the fantail of that destroyer, and I thought I had it made as a preacher or a teacher. One or the other.

"We got to Midway Island; truce was declared. You couldn't teach a guy to put a Band-Aid on. And you sure couldn't get him to go to church. All these reborn guys disappeared on me right there at Midway."

The *Sigourney* crossed the Pacific and hit Singapore and Hong Kong. Ensign Perot, since he didn't drink, became the permanent shore-patrol officer. He found himself pulling sailors out of whorehouses from the Malay Peninsula to Bangkok. They spent Christmas in Hong Kong and had a big party for the orphans on the ship.

They were at sea for six months when they pulled into South Korea. The sailors went on shore leave on Saturday night, and Perot's job was to bring them back on Sunday.

"That wasn't pretty, because they were in bad shape," he recalls. "They'd be tattooed and drunk. We'd spread them out on deck—let them sleep on deck because it was hot and they'd be sick—and as we'd clear the breakwater, the spray would start coming over the bow of the ship and they'd start going below."

When the *Sigourney* reached the Mediterranean Sea, the sailors were struck by the beauty of the women on the beach. "These guys were ready for liberty," Perot reminisces. "I hauled more guys out of jail in the next two or three days than I ever will in my life. One guy got drunk and decided to streak down the beach. I got a call to go and pick him up. It was a very funny sight, a young naval officer chasing a naked guy on the beach. I had no choice but to get the guy. And when I got him, I needed to do something with him, so I took off my officer's coat and wrapped it around his middle. We managed to get him back on the ship, but it must have appeared that there was a naked American officer running around the Riviera.

"But my great desire was to see a yacht. This was

my first chance. I wanted to go to the yacht basin and see the fun. See what the fuss was about.

"See, I grew up where ordinary people went to picnics and ran and played and had fun. So I could hardly wait to see what people did that had the ultimate toy. And it was a big shock when I got to the basin at Villefranche. The rich people were all sitting there in the yacht basin on their expensive boats, bored to death."

It was, if nothing else, an affirmation of something that his father told him as a boy. "Son," his father said, "material things aren't so important. Not at all. It's a lot more fun anticipating something than actually getting it."

Things are, after all, just things, he discovered, gazing at the bored yachtsmen along the Riviera. Quality is something far more precious and elusive.

5

"I still have his letters, much to his chagrin. He just hates the fact that I've got those letters. He wouldn't want them to get anywhere. Not so much what they say, but that they were written by a very young man and he wouldn't say things that way today. When you read them, and I take them out from time to time, you can see they were the letters of a young man. I don't care. I can't bear to throw them away. He wrote me these long, lovely letters. And he wrote often. He told me everything he saw and everything he did. His adventures. His impressions. And he told me what happened in Port Said."

—MARGOT PEROT

He wrote Margot letters at sea, sitting at a desk in his cabin, with her picture in a frame before him. She keeps the letters wrapped in ribbon, and they tell more than he might like to reveal of those early cruises when he was a young naval officer, filled with colorful stories about his visits to foreign countries and ports. The *Sigourney* had left its home port of Norfolk in June of 1953, then stopped at San Diego, Pearl Harbor, and Japan. It escorted the U.S.S. *Wisconsin* to Korea before beginning the second leg to Hong Kong and Singapore. After passing through the Suez Canal, in the spring of 1954, the destroyer sailed into the harbor of Port Said in Egypt. It was a time when the earth's political pot boiled with schemes and fetid intrigue and steamy gamesmanship. Egyptians were toying with the affections of both the East and the West—batting a coy eye for the Russians, dropping an inviting veil for the Americans, trifling heavily with the British, who were about to lose the Suez Canal to the wave of nationalism.

When the *Sigourney* arrived in the Egyptian harbor, there was one of those ubiquitous Russian trawlers, the kind loaded from the waterline to the top deck with sophisticated electronic gear. "They kept spying on the ship, spying on us," said Ross, remembering how annoyed the crew was at the encounter.

The Americans stared back in defiance at the Russians, then figured out a way to have a little of what they regarded as harmless fun with their Soviet tormentors.

The sailors playfully turned on their fire-control

system to frighten the Soviets; it set off a frenzied reaction on the radars and detection gear of the Russians. The Russian scopes and alarms lit up like Christmas trees. And then, as the American guns swung into action and swiveled in their turrets and pointed directly at the Russians, the enemy panicked.

"Oh, those guys hit the deck," recalled Ross Perot. "They jumped overboard. Did every damn thing in the world. We almost got in trouble on that."

It wasn't simply a high-spirited prank, however. The Americans, and in particular Perot, were frustrated. To understand why they tweaked the nose of the bear, one has to return to something that happened even earlier, as they came into the harbor. It was something Perot saw when the ship berthed. It was the unbelievable sight of black African slaves in chains being loaded onto ships for Arabian countries. Perot was horrified. He was on the bridge with the captain, Commander B. A. Lienhard. "I turned to the captain, I said, 'Aren't we going to do something about that?'

"The captain looked at me with a very sad face, and he said, 'We can't.' This was a slave ship with black slaves in manacles! This was in 1954!"

It was one of those moments that remain fresh and raw in the foreground of Ross Perot's memories. He keeps things like that handy, for lessons about life, and uses them to make a point, whips them out the way you'd pull out a snapshot for proof in an argument. He couldn't save the African slaves from being loaded onto the ship and delivered to Arabia, and it continued to bother him down through the years. He's aware it may sound corny or naïve, but Ross Perot believed that America stood for virtue and in-the-nick-of-time rescues. He thought he could do just about anything in the name of morality. That's what his parents taught him. And that's what they taught him at Annapolis, where they spent a lot of time drumming in lessons about honor and virtue. Now, he was forced to witness the degradation of his fellow humans, who were being loaded onto a slave ship. It was a bitter —almost impossible—thing for him to swallow.

"I just assumed we could do something."

Some could interpret this as the high-handed arrogance of a callow young man. But there is that other, more generous, explanation, which is that he is imbued with a deep sense of responsibility. Why else would Ross Perot display such personal and intense liability for the moral behavior within his own universe? Why is he constrained always to act on his convictions while others feather and debate? This second possibility tells why he was willing to turn on the fire-control systems and level the guns of an American warship, the U.S.S. *Sigourney*, at a Russian vessel. It also demonstrates why he was unwilling to abandon, for the sake of some larger, abstract political benefit, American POWs in Vietnam. And this may be why it was inevitable that at a later stage of his life he was bound to go after his company employees held captive in Iran.

Such moral absolutes were planted in those long, languorous conversations on horseback on the plains of Texarkana, when he rode with his father on their beloved Tennessee walkers. His father told stories and explained the lessons of life in his quiet, clear manner; the instruction that lingered in the mind of Ross Perot was that a man cannot turn away from injustice.

"You can't just stand by, Ross," his father would say. "A man has got to put in his two cents or he isn't worth the price of his dinner."

These were powerful lectures. They colored Perot's youth like an unbroken fable. He speaks of his childhood lyrically. They sat united around a wooden console radio, he recalls mistily, and listened to *Fibber McGee and Molly* and *Amos 'n' Andy*. They were all together when they heard in shock and amazement World War II actually break out on their own radio. It was on the Gabriel Heatter news program. The announcer's voice echoes still: "He said, 'There's bad news tonight,'" says Ross. "I can still hear him saying it."

And he can still see his father, who got up at six every morning, standing at the kitchen counter, eating his breakfast before he went out to face the duties that a salesman had to face. And every day at noon his father was home for lunch, and every evening at six he was home for dinner. And the meals did not start until he bowed his head for a prayer: "Gracious Father, make us thankful for all these blessings we humbly ask, for Christ's sake, Amen."

No matter how old he would grow, he could hear the sound of his mother's voice, endlessly reading aloud from children's stories like *The Little Engine That Could*, or repeating timeless aphorisms about the nature of goodness and evil and the moral obligation to adhere to the former. He was captivated by her uncompromising stance about leaving intact the mark in front of her house, inviting the half-starved beggars from the trains in for a meal: "Let it be," she said simply, ending all debate. Ross Perot would never forget.

Ross Perot enjoyed the sea. He liked the pitch and the roll of a voyage and the neat, orderly, compact style of a well-run ship. And he enjoyed the camaraderie among the sailors. As he told an interviewer more than thirty years later, "When you're at sea for a year, that's like ten years of short cruises. There were three hundred of us on board. We were together in cramped quarters twenty-four hours a day, and we were at sea for six and seven weeks at a time. That's the best practical experience in management and leadership that I could have gotten anywhere in the world."

What he didn't like was the navy. He wanted out. "It was too confining," he says. "Promotions were based on seniority, there was nothing you could do to push it along, no matter how good you were. Nothing based on merit. It took years to move up a rank. I did not like that one bit. I liked the sea and the ships and the men. But the navy was frozen in cement."

He was restless, and not cut out for that kind of regimentation. His grievances became specific when the *Sigourney* changed captains after that first worldwide voyage. Ross Perot got in trouble for the same reason he always seems to get in trouble: hard-nosed, stubborn, cussed righteous pride. The immovable object (Ross Perot) came up against the irresistible force (navy habits of privilege and perks).

When the *Sigourney* went back to sea in 1954, Ross Perot didn't get along with a new senior officer assigned to the destroyer. According to Perot, the officer was an old salt, set in his ways, who thought that he was entitled to some extra perks. Perot says that he was ordered to use the crew's recreation funds to redesign the officer's sea cabin. He refused. When the same senior officer asked Perot to supply him with liquor from the medicinal whiskey store (which was in Perot's charge), Perot again said no. (The ship's commander at the time was Gerald Scott, who has denied any conflict took place with Perot.)

Perot applied for a transfer, and in 1955 he reported to the aircraft carrier U.S.S. *Leyte*, as assistant navigation officer.

Ross sulked for a while, then complained to his father, who, though near death, took up his son's cause and wrote two letters to the then-sitting Texas senators asking for help in getting his son an early release from the service. It was a breach of his incorruptible rectitude—openly seeking a favor—but it seemed to a lot of his friends that young Perot was suffering considerably. Moreover, no great crime was involved here. His father was merely entreating his senators to act on what he viewed as a legitimate grievance.

"Ross has now served two years in the Navy and has sent in his resignation asking for release from active duty and a transfer into the reserves," his father wrote to Senator Price Daniel on July 11, 1955. The letter went on to say that Ross had made up his mind against attempting to fashion a career in the navy and asked for intervention for an early release through the secretary of the navy. A comparable letter was sent to Lyndon Johnson, then a senator. Nothing came of these entreaties, and later that year Ross's father died and Ross's longing to leave the navy subsided, mitigated, no doubt, by his overwhelming grief. He was with his father when he died, and Ross senior's death left his son dulled and sad.

In January of 1956, after meeting with the chief of naval personnel, Admiral James Holloway, Jr., Ross withdrew his request for an early discharge. (He claims now that it was a misunderstanding,

that he was under the impression that he was obli-
gated to serve for two years rather than four, and
since the Korean conflict as well as the national
emergency was over, he saw no point in staying beyond his obligatory two-year term. Nevertheless, he
did complete the four-year stint, was promoted to
full lieutenant, honorably discharged, and served an
additional five years in the Naval Reserve.)

It was Margot who pulled him out of the doldrums.
    When Ross's father died and he flew home on
emergency leave, Margot flew down to Texarkana
for the funeral. That gesture alone seemed to settle
once and for all the question of their enduring relationship. "It meant a lot to the family when Margot
came down," recalls Bette.
    They were wed at the First Presbyterian Church
in Greensburg, Pennsylvania, on September 15,
1956. It was an afternoon affair, with some three
hundred guests, and the dance and reception
were at the country club. Ross wore his navy uniform.
    Margot sensed from the tone and texture of
Ross's letters what kind of man she was getting. "I
knew that I could trust him," she said. "I knew that
he was strong and honest. I knew that much. And I

knew that life would never be dull if he was around. It may not sound romantic, but it was. He was an overwhelming presence."

When Margot graduated from Goucher College, she taught grade-school classes at the McDonogh School, then a military boys' school near Baltimore. She was enchanted by being surrounded by all those attentive boys in uniform trying to act grown up. "I loved it," she recalls. "I had twenty-five little boys in the third grade. I probably would've kept on there—definitely would've stayed on there—if I hadn't gotten married in the fall."

Margot had adored her father and was conscious of the fact that she was exchanging one powerful man in her life—her father—for another, Ross. Her father was forty-eight when she was born, but he wielded great influence over his daughter. "I remember sitting outside with him in the evening, and he would tell stories. We'd all gather around, and he'd make up this wonderful story about a make-believe character called Morty and his magic pocket handkerchief. I can still see him smoking his cigar and talking about Morty and how he'd make himself invisible with his magic handkerchief. Of course my father was interested in politics, so he'd go everywhere with the magic handkerchief that made him invisible. The political conventions, everywhere. The next night the adventure would continue."

This was not unlike the intense and playful bonding that took place in the Perot household. They might have come from different parts of the country, but the substance of the Birmingham and Perot families was the same.

Although Margot did not know her father's first wife (she died in the flu epidemic of 1919), her mother, Gertrude Price, was a role model for the young girl. Gertrude and Donald had been friends because she banked at the Hazelwood Savings & Trust Company, where he was president. "She was a chemistry major and very bright," recalls Margot. "She helped the students at Johns Hopkins. Somebody would say, 'Miss Price, you have a caller,' and it was always somebody who needed help in organic chemistry. She did work for the Mellon Institute for a while in Pittsburgh. She later taught Latin at a private school."

Gertrude Price Birmingham was a graduate of Goucher, class of '22. Margot is convinced that in a later era Gertrude would have been a doctor like her father, instead of a chemistry clerk.

Margot was pleased when she realized she had a

gift for teaching. But, strangely, she discovered something else after her marriage. "I was very happy as a navy wife," she says. "I enjoyed the other wives and the society of the navy. And I was very proud of Ross."

They rented a small, one-bedroom furnished apartment—seventy-five dollars a month—in Wickford, Rhode Island, so they could be near his duty station at the Quonset Naval Air Station. Wickford was a town for walking, the neighbors were friendly, and teaching was satisfying. Their three-room apartment was crowded with wedding presents—silver, china, bowls.

"I had the greatest mother-in-law," Margot says. "She always took my side. First thing she would say is, 'Ross, now that you have all these nice presents, you have to get Margot a house to put them in.' And whenever we had a disagreement, she'd say that I was right."

Periodically, Ross would be gone at sea for a while, and all his homecomings became honeymoons. "We saved money," Margot Perot recalls. "I put all my salary in a savings account. Because we just didn't need it. We didn't spend much at all. The movies on the base were ten cents. And we'd go to the Officers' Club for dinner and not spend much. We'd buy what we needed and didn't worry. We had one car [a 1952 Plymouth], and we were happy. We didn't have a television, and we didn't care."

"We lived in a house so old that the owners got their title originally from the Indians," Ross laughs.

Margot remembers Ross buying a Heath Kit to build a stereo system. "He had it all spread out, all this stuff, and then he'd go out to sea—and I didn't know what to do with it." It stayed in the middle of the table while he was at sea. She would stare at the parts, wondering if clutter would be a part of the decor. He was gone for a month, and then, when the ship came into Quonset Point, she went to meet it. "I went to Quonset Point, driving down to Narragansett Bay until I caught sight of the ship coming in, and it was so exciting," she says. "The band would be playing, and all the wives and little children would be there. Everybody waiting. And Ross would bring that ship in. I was so impressed with that. I've probably been more impressed with that than lots of other accomplishments. You'd see this huge ship being docked, and you knew that he was giving the orders because although he was the assistant navigator, the navigator used to say, 'Well,

Perot, you bring it in.' And then I thought of the living-room floor with the pieces of the hi-fi system scattered from one end of the room to the other."

Life aboard the *Leyte* was not unpleasant, especially for a man of Ross Perot's boundless energy. But in 1957, he began thinking of a civilian job.

"And one day on the *Leyte*, we had all these guests on the bridge," Perot says. "The secretary of the navy. VIPs. They all come on board. And I'm in charge. Well, one of the guests was an IBM executive who was intrigued. We had these nine destroyers around us, in a protective screen I was launching and landing airplanes, I was reorienting the destroyer screen, I was bringing fuel and ammunition ships alongside.

"So he was impressed that this kid was doing all that. And the captain said, 'Well, he's getting out of the navy pretty soon.' And the IBM executive came over and said, 'Son, would you like to have an interview with IBM?' And I'll never forget, I looked him in the eye, I said, 'Mister, you bet I'd like to have an interview with your company.'

"I said, 'I've worked since I was seven years old,

and I'm twenty-seven now, and you're the first person in my life to ever offer me a job.' I always had to look for work. I said, 'Yes, sir, I really would like to have an interview with your company. And I don't even know what you do.' "

6

"For years I'd say I'd be going home, and I meant Pennsylvania. I was a little afraid of Texas. The size. That's what I first saw in 1957. It was during the big drought. It was absolutely flat and brown. And I wondered where people went for a Sunday drive. There wasn't anything you'd want to look at. It's changed since that time, thank goodness. We don't have those droughts. And now my roots are here and I love it."

—MARGOT PEROT

There was never any doubt about the fertility of the ground of Texas for Ross Perot. Even when temptations were dangled for him to move to greener pastures, he dug in his heels and fought for Texas. There was no doubt that he wanted to live and work in Texas. When Margot was convinced, or at least persuaded, that her future lay in the Lone Star State, Ross had to sway the IBM management.

He breezed through the aptitude test, but the IBM recruiters were astonished at his mulish stance about where he worked. Most candidates were simply grateful for an offer from the blue-chip, cutting-edge business-machine company. But then, there was a lot about Ross Perot that didn't fit the IBM pattern. It might have been predictable, considering his open and guileless attitude when he met the IBM executive aboard the U.S.S. *Leyte*; he made no bones about his ignorance of the company's business.

Recalling that first shipboard encounter, Ross says: "He asked me again, because it was kinda odd, and I said we've got some IBM typewriters on the ship. So he told me about computers and what have you, and I said that I was still eager for an opportunity, and he laughed and said come ahead. So I drove to Hartford, Connecticut, for my first interview."

He must have impressed personnel, because IBM offered him a job right away. But then came that nonnegotiable Texas demand. They wanted him in Connecticut. Ross wanted to work in Texas.

"They said, 'No, we want you up here.' I said, 'I'd rather work in Texas.' Finally they said, 'Okay, we'll get you another interview in Texas,' and I got a job in Dallas."

Ross and Margot didn't have a lot of possessions

when they packed up in the summer of 1957 for the move south. They could fit everything that they owned in the trunk and backseat of their 1952 Plymouth. The fact that they owned virtually nothing did not seem like a particularly daunting hardship.

"I believe that we were as happy back then as we are today," she says simply, thirty-five years later, sitting in her Georgian mansion in Dallas. On the wall is an Impressionist painting by Claude Monet. On the opposite wall is a Renoir. The house is filled with antique vases, precious screens, rare paintings, valuable rugs. Outside, sprinkled amid the rolling acres of the select North Dallas estate, there is a tennis court, a swimming pool, a man-made waterfall (the dam constructed by Ross himself), and a brook running across the grounds. There are horses in the stables, groundskeepers working on the immaculate lawns, and private guards in white shirts and gray slacks with 9-millimeter guns on their hips patrolling the borders discreetly.

Recalling that earlier time, however, Ross is in full agreement with his wife. "We couldn't have been happier. Material things have nothing to do with happiness. We literally started with nothing."

Spartan and frugal, Ross had adopted his father's

minimalist philosophy. Quoting Ross senior, he recalls: "He said, 'Son, nobody ever went broke with
money in the bank. So if you want something, save
your money and then buy it.' And he told me as a
little boy, he said, 'Now I'm going to tell you something you'll see as true: Looking forward to owning
it is probably better than having it.' So he said that
the nicest part of saving your money for something
is the anticipation. 'Once you've got it, it's there.' "

Margot, who didn't have a washing machine or a
dryer, who went down to the Laundromat to do her
wash, and who never had a new stove until 1964,
when she was a multimillionaire, agreed whole-
heartedly with her husband's views about money.
"Those things didn't seem to matter much," she
says.

"We paid cash for everything," he says. "We
bought used appliances, always paid cash, always
saved our money, always had money in the bank.
Pretty simple, right? We figured nobody was going
to look after us but us. So if we ever had a crisis,
we'd be prepared."

Margot has even cast their early financial strug-
gles in a somewhat sentimental light.

"Our first apartment in Dallas, now that was
something," she recalls. "We'd set a budget. We

had a limit of a hundred dollars for rent. We kept seeing these apartments that were too expensive. They'd be one thirty-five or one twenty-five. And finally we found one that we couldn't resist. It was wonderful, an apartment with two bedrooms and a living room and a dining room and a sun porch. It was just open and airy and near everything that we wanted to be near. It was a duplex. We were downstairs. There was another couple upstairs. And so Ross volunteered to cut the grass, trim the hedges, make some minor repairs, and take care of the building so we could get it down to one-ten.

"And then we started buying furniture. . . ."

Ross went through the IBM training course with ease. He instinctively knew how to be a salesman. And he became a believer in the future of computer power; IBM engineers were far out in front of competitors in developing business machines and adapting them for office use. Another thing that appealed to Ross was that IBM salesmen were buttoned-down types in dark suits and clean white shirts and neckties. The crispness of their manner seemed to reflect the solid efficiency of the machines that they sold. They seemed to represent a new breed of business warrior, incapable of failure.

It was a time when mainframe computers were revolutionizing white-collar work. Even the literature and culture of that age reflected an edgy uncertainty about the dehumanizing effect that machines and automation would bring to the workplace. The movie *Desk Set* had as its chief villain a computer. And it wasn't only the infallibility of the machines. *The Man in the Gray Flannel Suit* reflected an underlying reservation about the benign nature of the coming corporate culture.

None of that daunted Ross Perot, who, as a dedicated rationalist and an unfailing optimist, believed in getting the job done. "I am totally focused. When I have something to do I do it. I don't like to get too heavy with this philosophical stuff."

And so he went out plugging the IBM 1401, the commercial workhorse of that era. By modern computer-chip standards, it was a clumsy, inefficient lummox of a machine, the size of a small closet, which could hold a few thousand words in its small memory bank. But in spite of that, during those early computer days, it was seen as a marvel and could handle the workload of a dozen clerks.

In his book *Perot*, Todd Mason describes the apprentice technician soaking up information and data like a human computer chip. Perot locked himself alone in a room and studied, and when he came out, he dazzled his superiors with his energy and drive, even moving a cot into the computer room of a trucking firm during a particularly difficult installation. Mason quotes a former partner who witnessed the indefatigable Perot feeding punch cards into the computer all through the night: "Right away you think: This guy is not run of the mill."

It was the custom of IBM—a company founded on hard-sell principles by Thomas J. Watson—to encourage its sales force to greater efforts by binding its commissions to the satisfaction of the customer. The salesmen received half of their commission on signing and half after a lengthy installation and acceptance period. Thus, the salesmen had a stake not only in selling a machine to a customer, but an equal interest in making certain that the customer was happy.

Perot naturally drew the hardest accounts. This suited his feisty style, harking back to the days when he rode horseback through the unpaved streets of Texarkana on a newspaper route that no one else wanted. One of the problem accounts was the Southwestern Life Insurance Company, which Perot had signed up to buy a $1.3-million IBM 7070, the largest commercial machine of the time. But

Southwestern didn't really need that much capacity. "It's like if you had a bulldozer and used it for one and a half shifts and then it sat idle for one and a half shifts—why not sell the unused shifts." This was Perot's flash of inspiration.

Time-sharing. Get someone else to foot a piece of the cost of the computer for shared-time use. Frantically, Perot tried to match up another company with the 7070 to see if he could find one that needed the mainframe and would help handle the cost. He struck it lucky. He found a Dallas-based government agency, the Agricultural Commodity Price Stabilization Service, which was sending computer technicians to New Orleans each week to rent time on a 7070 there. Why not save the airplane fare and travel time and use the downtime from the Southwestern computer?

Everyone else in the office was skeptical, but Ross closed the deal with precision and irrefutable math. He fashioned a deal in which all the parties saved money, and he landed his big commission.

Meanwhile, in 1958, Margot became pregnant. Rather than phone, Ross and Margot drove over to Texarkana, and on the porch where the family used to sit in the evening over peach ice cream, they informed Lulu May Perot that she was about to become a grandmother.

As it turned out, on the day that Ross junior was born—November 7, 1958—Lulu May moved out of the house on Olive Street in Texarkana. When Ross tried to call her to tell her the news that she had her first grandchild, he couldn't reach her.

"He couldn't get me, either, because I was helping her move to Fort Worth," says Bette. "I was in Texarkana at my grandmother Ray's home, and the call came. We got the things in the car and drove straight to Baylor Hospital, and she saw the baby that night. Her first grandchild."

They spent Christmas together at the Perot apartment. "I have a strong memory on Christmas Eve of Mother and Margot bent over that little baby who was a little more than a month old, peering at him, being sure that he was all right."

And so all the Christmases afterward were spent at Ross's home and all the Thanksgivings at Bette's. "Margot really enjoyed having the Santa Claus and the children at her home," Bette recalls.

Q: Who played Santa?
A: Ross and Margot.
Q: Did they dress up?

A: Oh, no, no. But their children certainly believed in Santa Claus.

Meanwhile, by 1961, things were going awry for Perot at IBM. IBM instituted a new plan, which might have been devised especially to thwart Perot. Each salesman was given a yearly quota for commissions. The moment he met his quota, he was no longer eligible to earn additional commissions on sales. This was designed to prevent hotshot salesmen from outearning their sales managers.

Ross didn't like it. He had plans for pushing the product, earning money above and beyond the commission system. He tried to take the shared-time idea and expand it into a separate department of the company. But the IBM managers, whose profits largely stemmed from hardware, didn't see any future in software maintenance, or in redirecting the emphasis of the company. The attitude reminded Ross Perot of naval-style management: paralysis.

The signal event, and a deflating one it was, came after his biggest sale. On January 19, 1962, Perot sold a state-of-the-art IBM 7090 to the Graduate Research Center of the Southwest, thus meeting his yearly quota. He had no further incentives to do any more work. To drive home his point, he began bringing a towel and a bathing suit into the office, suggesting that he might as well go swimming for the rest of the year.

"It was so easy to sell IBM equipment then that I wasn't having any trouble at all exceeding my quota," he told an interviewer. "I told them, 'Look, the only thing I'm doing different from the other salesmen is that I work all day and they don't.' "

He then made IBM a bold offer, according to the *Dallas City* magazine. "I told them it was okay with me if they promoted me and paid me less money, or if they could pay me a smaller commission than the other salesmen. But I had to stay busy. I couldn't stand being idle. Well, I never dreamed they would accept my suggestion. That was the biggest mistake of my business career. They actually did it! They cut my commission by eighty percent!"

There were some attempts to make accommodations. He asked for a promotion; he was sent to Los Angeles to consider a job as a sales manager. The cultural differences aside, he declined the offer. "If I stayed, I would have become a gray, middle-management problem," he says.

One Saturday morning, when the future looked as flat and bleak as that first sight of the Texas landscape did to Margot, Ross was waiting for his turn in the barber chair at a shop in North Dallas. He glanced through a well-thumbed *Reader's Digest*. It was the December 1961 issue. He found, at the bottom of the page, one of those short inspirational homilies used by the magazine to send commercial soldiers back into the breach of commercial battle aroused with new fire. It was a quotation from Henry David Thoreau: "The mass of men lead lives of quiet desperation."

"I said, 'There I am; that's me.' And I decided I had to try to make my ideas work on my own."

7

"Capitalism works. It's better than any other system."

—ROSS PEROT

Of course capitalism worked for an itchy autocrat like Ross Perot who could not abide the painful crawl to the top required in the military with its mandarin traditions, or the obsequious grind to fit into the mold of the American corporation. This small, tidy, immaculate man, who walked like a rooster with his head stretched to the utmost limit, as if he were reaching for some far boundary of his potential, had a volatility that could not be contained by the usual rules of success. He was aching to explode.

And yet, contrary to popular myth, he was not the reckless merchant gunfighter, shooting from the lip, when he set out to launch his own company. At first he tried to do it through the approved channels of the parent company, IBM, although deep down, he must have suspected that it couldn't be done; when he attempted to float his innovative approach to computer marketing to his superiors, it landed like cement. Still, Perot tried.

He called his concept "facilities management," and the solution to the waste of computer-hardware capacity and management of time was, as they say when describing complex equations in higher mathematics, "elegant." IBM, Perot suggested, should lease the hardware to a customer, then send in its own software teams, who would install it, maintain it, and operate it. In that way, the customer wouldn't have to learn computerspeak or retrain all company employees to become computer hackers (in addition to their specific fields of expertise). So a bank could concentrate on banking, while the computer specialists handled the machines. A trucking company would keep on trucking, and so forth.

But the IBM development people scoffed at Perot's notion, and the high executives made belittling remarks about the insignificant earning potential of such an odd venture. They'd achieved dominance with hardware—things that they could see and touch, plastic and metal. What Perot was suggesting was an abstraction, something almost metaphysically impossible for the bottom-line people to grasp. So Ross Perot decided to do it on his own, albeit cautiously, with lots of safety nets and complete faith in his own capacity to recover from any possible failure.

The idea had timely sizzle because of the chaotic state of the computer universe at that hour. Companies all across the country, fearful of becoming obsolete in the information age, were buying high-tech machinery they didn't know how to use, just to keep up with the competition. Once they had upgraded and modernized, many were perplexed: They didn't know how to take full advantage of their big costly machines. They were more than simply bewildered, they were panicked. They had spent a fortune and didn't have a clue about these megabyte monsters eating up their numbers and spitting out spreadsheets and blinking back with the acurser eye. They needed to lean on a user-friendly shoulder.

Perot offered his. He would take the burden off their hands instantly, not after years of frustration, false starts, retraining, and study. His staff would move in, analyze the company, design systems tailored to the specific needs of the customer, install the hardware, and put experts in to manage the system. All the customer had to do was to sign a long-term contract with Perot.

He had prepared the ground carefully. Though naturally high-strung and impatient, Perot was an agreeable salesman in a Texas, good-ole-boy kind of way. He learned to make small talk, attended dinner parties, traded jokes. Still, he never broke promises he made to his father about smoking and drinking. There were wisecracks and jests about his sanctimonious abstention, but then he shrugged off all criticism as a waste of time. Perot did not suffer afterthoughts. He had his ways, and he was going to stick to them.

He and Margot had a burgeoning nest egg—her salary had always gone directly into the bank—and he wrote a check for one thousand dollars, which was the fee for incorporating in Texas. (Thus began the legend of the gargantuan company being capitalized on a thousand-dollar shoestring. Today, the check sits under glass, along with many other trophies, in his North Dallas office.) Actually, he had more than just a small amount of money in the bank. In addition to the commissions from IBM, which were still coming in, along with his yearly salary for 1962, he held a part-time job as a consulting data-processing manager for Blue Cross–Blue

Shield of Texas, Inc. He had his own office, for which he paid rent of one hundred dollars a month, and a secretary in the Blue Cross building in downtown Dallas.

But when he tried to get outside investors to provide additional capital, he came up blank. "I took the idea around to all the people who would normally finance a new venture, and none of them thought it would work," he told *Dallas City* magazine. "I was stuck with the whole thing. . . . Nobody else wanted it."

He put his wife, his mother, and his sister on the board of directors; the Perot family was in business without an out.

"Every few months the navy sent me letters asking me to come back," Perot recalled. "There I was, running around, trying to sell an interest in a company that nobody wanted, and the navy stopped sending me letters right after I started EDS. When I called navy personnel to find out why, they said, 'We don't want you anymore; you're over thirty-two.' So there went my escape hatch. Now, I had to make this business work."

And so, as on all events he counts as auspicious, he picked June 27, 1962—his birthday—to incorporate Electronic Data Systems (EDS). It amused him later, when he had his own building and put the name of the company on the front, that a lot of people looked at the letters "EDS" and thought someone named Ed had opened a restaurant.

As in most things, Ross Perot had definite opinions about how to run his company. First, his salesmen would be neat, well-dressed, and would not show up on a job with facial hair. After all, they were competing with IBM, whose conservative management style practically invented the buttoned-down man, topped by a snap-brim hat. (EDS eliminated the hat.) There were other vital requirements for employment—some that went deep into that well-spring of values he picked up as a child.

"He'd say, about infidelity, that it wasn't a matter of morality," recalls Morton Meyerson, one of the early Perot protégés who later became president of the company as well as a millionaire under Perot's tutelage. "It was a matter of if you'll cheat on your wife, you'll cheat the company, and you'll cheat the customer."

But that was only partly true. There were tenets he held that stood like the Alamo. Ross Perot believed that adultery was wrong, and it always bothered him when people made excuses for it. The link between sin and practical problems made company policy convenient to justify.

The same thing was true of the dress code. It became a happy coincidence of pragmatism and conviction. "I don't think it had anything to do with clothing per se," recalls Meyerson. "It had everything to do with what we wanted to portray to the customers so they would have confidence in us."

This was the sixties, the early days of computers, and the typical hacker was an odd duck, eccentric in his ways. "They were hippielike people," recalls Meyerson. "And senior executives of the bank would come down to the data-processing department and find people wearing thongs and blue jeans and T-shirts, wearing beads with long hair and smoking marijuana. Now you can imagine what they thought of that. So EDS shows up with guys in blue suits and white shirts and short hair, with a military bearing. They had greater confidence in those people."

The code of ethics, the dress code, the behavior regulations, were all, as Perot likes to say now, "buzzwords."

"It's kind of like high school football," he told an interviewer. ". . . The thing I love is, if you read the press clippings, you would think that we were a very formal, very stiff organization. The facts are we [were] very informal, very close, a very warm organization."

And where did he find his cadre? Perot had a couple of critical suppliers of bright, willing, and upright candidates. One was the military; it's no surprise that an early Perot hiree was Milledge Hart III, an Annapolis graduate who would later be named president of EDS. Perot recruiters would scout the military bases for talent—and there was no shortage. And then there was IBM. He raided his old company—he always greatly admired much about IBM, referring to it as "the Delta Force of corporate America"—for gifted technicians. "He really did pick over the office," Perot's former sales manager, James Campbell, has said. "He was able to identify the very best."

Perot had a decided gift for choosing men and women. He fostered a high esprit de corps and built an organization more like an elite unit of commandos than a band of white-collar hackers. He wrote his motto boldly on the wall: "Eagles don't flock; you have to find them one at a time." And Perot wanted everyone who worked for him to consider himself an eagle.

But regardless of how talented his help, they'd be useless unless EDS could locate other firms in need of computer assistance. Perot started out in June; and by October he was hitting a money crunch. Sales call after sales call came up cold. But on the seventy-ninth try, the Collins Radio Company in Cedar Rapids, Iowa, agreed to Perot's offer. On Friday evenings, an army of Collins's programmers descended upon Dallas to take over the Southwestern computer system until Sunday night, managing Collins Radio's affairs. Perot was able to put $100,000 in the bank, and he soon began recruiting more systems engineers.

Still, this was treading financial water. It wasn't until February 13, 1963, that Perot landed his first big account. And it wasn't a computer chip, but a potato chip, that made him solvent. The snack food company Frito-Lay was trying to develop a precision sales-route accounting system. The Frito-Lay people had already ordered a large IBM computer when Perot convinced them it wasn't necessary. His people would do the work on rented machines and save Frito-Lay the huge capital costs.

In retrospect, Perot was flying by the seat of his pants. He raided his old company, and he sold the pick of the programmers on the idea that he had a year's salary for them in the bank and that he was compensating them with stock that would one day be valuable, but for now—well, they would have to trust him so that he could have operating capital. And they believed him. He put them to work on long-term projects and pledged his word, and that was good enough for most of those who had known him in the service or at IBM.

Perot tried to imbue his staff with a sense of mission. Yes, they would work hard and stretch the limits of their capacities, but they could be in on the ground floor of something exciting, something with infinite potential. And so the programmers and salesmen came, despite the frustrations and hardships. They were like an army of night crawlers, driving from mainframe computer to computer, wherever they could scrounge some free time, inputting their feasibility studies, drawing up models for routes and expected returns. Working harder than they did at IBM for less money but, somehow, convinced that they would be adequately remunerated.

Perot tried to make up for the endless days and lost weekends. Every year he held a black-tie dinner for his employees. He also staged a company picnic at his summer home at Grapevine Lake. He visited wives and thanked them for their patience and handed them one hundred shares of stock, which didn't seem like much when it was then selling at $16 a share, but would in time be worth about $400,000. His personal touches and generosity are well remembered. He observed employees' anniversaries and children's birthdays. When one of his managers' wives splashed drain cleaner in her eye, he got a leading ophthalmologist to care for her. And when another manager's son was born with a congenital heart defect, he rounded up a leading cardiac surgeon to perform corrective surgery. He was there when children were sick and needed medical help or when family members died. "People I work with are just like family," Perot says. "I feel very strongly for them. They don't just work here—I love them."

Morton Meyerson first glimpsed Ross Perot in 1964, when he attended a data-processing management meeting in Dallas. Meyerson was, at the time, a twenty-six-year-old hotshot computer whiz fresh out of the army, then working for Bell Helicopters. It was the dawn of America's intervention in South Vietnam and the military-technology buildup was already under way. Meyerson wanted to be a player in that looming computer explosion.

"I was at this convention, and I saw Ross give a talk," he recalls. "I remember how small he was—he appeared to be kind of fragile. Some people might even describe him as ordinary. There's nothing striking about his looks. Yet, when he spoke, he had enormous power. His ability to communicate was the best I'd ever seen. And he was talking about technical matters. Talking about issues that would be important to data-processing people—professionals. But I never talked to him; I just listened. Well, a year and a half later I was promoted to the parent company of Bell Helicopter, Textron. My wife, Marlene, and I were getting ready to move from Fort Worth to Providence, Rhode Island, when I got a call from this company, EDS. Never heard of them."

The pitch came from Mitch Hart, Perot's old Annapolis classmate, and Meyerson was smitten by the sense of promise and broad horizons. He took the job, but he never saw his ultimate boss, except at a distance. After he was with the company for eight months, though, he and Perot locked horns. Meyerson had been hired along with two other Bell Helicopter people, and all three were working on a

Perot's 1953 Naval Academy yearbook photograph.

Ross on horseback (1947).

His parents, Gabriel Ross and Lulu May,
at home in Texarkana (1948).

Aboard the U.S.S. *Roan* in New York Harbor. Perot on deck taking his first look at Wall Street (1950).

And aboard the U.S.S. *Sigourney* (1953).

Aboard the U.S.S. *Missouri* (1952).

During his final year at the Naval Academy, Perot was recognized for leadership by Admiral C. Turner Joy (1953).

With parents and sister Bette at graduation (1953).

Perot and Dwight Eisenhower shake hands on the president's visit to the Naval Academy (1953).

With mother and fiancée, Margot Birmingham (1953).

Ross with new wife, Margot (1956).

Mr. and Mrs. Perot today.

Perot hosts a parade in Dallas for returned prisoners of war and the Son Tay Raiders (1973).

At a press conference with Colonel Arthur D. "Bull" Simon upon arrival in Dallas after the Iran rescue (1979).

EDS was first listed on the New York Stock Exchange in 1970.

In front of the Magna Carta at the National Archives (1984).

Perot receives the Winston Churchill Award
from Prince Charles (1984).

Perot bids son farewell before Ross junior's departure on a helicopter trip around the world (September 1982).

The Perot children (*from left*): Suzanne, Katherine, Ross junior, Nancy, and Carolyn.

Ross and Margot with their eldest daughter, Nancy, on her wedding day.

Ross with daughters Suzanne, Carolyn, Nancy, and Katherine (*left to right*).

project at the usual EDS pace—sixteen hours a day, seven days a week. They were taking meals on the fly and running on adrenaline. It was the sort of operation that weeded out the less than whole-hearted soldiers. The two other men quit.

"Ross called me directly himself and asked me if I would go have a cup of coffee with him across the street at the Eat Well Cafe on Lane Wood," Meyerson recalls. "We sat down, and he said, 'Mort, I understand that Jim and Rick are leaving the company.' I said, 'Yes, that's right.' And he said, 'Apparently, it's too tough for them.' And I said, 'Yes, that's right.' And he said, 'I'd like to get straight to the point with you—if you're going to leave the company with your friends, I'd like to know about it, because I'd like to face it directly. If you have gangrene in your toe, you cut off your toe, and you just face the music. I need to know where we stand.' "

A common characteristic among Perot personnel is a combination of stubborn pride and rock-hard grit. These are people who endure impossible hours, unheard-of demands, and the crisp commands of Ross Perot. Mort Meyerson had his own flinty side, which he was about to display to Ross Perot.

"I said, 'Ross, it kind of irritates me that you

bring that question to me. What you're basically asking is, Am I a pantywaist like my friends? I'll tell you what my answer is—I never quit in the middle of anything. I wouldn't resign from the company for anything until I finish the project. Unless you fire me. But once I finish the project, then I will make the decision about whether I'll stay or not.' And he said, 'Fine, that's fair.' And that was the end of our conversation."

But it was the beginning of an enduring and critical relationship. Ross Perot had found his war-horse. As he says today, "I picked Mort Meyerson because he's a troublemaker—he turns the world upside down and paints it pink."

8

> "It is a businessman's job to make a product that is wanted and sells in the marketplace. It must be sold aggressively. Now, all this may not sound interesting to some people who say, 'ho-hum,' but the truth is that there is no shortcut to creating jobs—no magic. It is fundamental business practice and imagination that creates jobs."
>
> —ROSS PEROT IN *THE SATURDAY EVENING POST*

Morton Meyerson, who was an ex-soldier working as an underpaid computer technician until he ran into Ross Perot, is sitting in the exclusive penthouse suite of a New York luxury hotel. He wears a cotton shirt and khaki slacks. He fends off calls from CEOs of other large companies to chat about his old boss and partner. He can afford to keep people waiting. At fifty-four, he is worth tens of millions of dollars.

"I worked hard," recalls Meyerson, who since his retirement from EDS has run his own consulting firm. "I did things I had no idea I could do. I remember when there were fifty of us. I remember when there were one hundred. And then I remember when it was five hundred, and five thousand, and then fifty thousand. Ross wasn't a whole bunch different. He grew, he matured, he got skinned knees, he learned from his mistakes. He had broader breadth. Scope. But his fundamental values were fixed and firm. No, he hasn't changed a bunch."

It is understandable that during those first years of EDS's existence Ross Perot worked like a demon, often putting in twenty-hour days, seven-day weeks, and generally moving at a high, feverish pitch to chase his customers and find idle computers to plunder. After all, he was trying to build his own business on little more than a smile and a shoe-string. But what is not so readily comprehensible, what raises his story above an Horatio Alger tale of reward and effort, is why all those other volunteers marched behind him at the same murderous pace.

Why did men who, for the most part, had little tangible stake in the duration of this eccentric idea, work all day at regular technical jobs in regular computer shops, then gather in their soldier-blue suits at Ross Perot's office at dusk and pick up the spools of data from clients and stuff them in their car trunks and scatter to the unused offices in the dark underbelly of Dallas and Fort Worth to write programs on borrowed computers? Why did they put up with grudging night watchmen, risky streets, low wages, and burn the candle until dawn so that Ross Perot's marginal enterprise could survive?

One clue was the recruitment policy. "I want people who are smart, tough, self-reliant, have a history of success since childhood, a history of being best at what they've done, people who love to win —and if you run out of people who love to win, look for people who hate to lose" was Perot's personnel credo.

There is another answer, an old one: that when people are lost in an uncharted forest of business bureaucracy and ambiguity they tend to follow someone who at least seems to know the way out of the woods. And Ross Perot gave every indication that he was no longer the assistant navigator on the U.S.S. *Leyte*—he now was the master of his own ship. Cecil Gunn, plucked away from IBM to staff the Frito-Lay account in 1964, attempted to describe the depth of the passion inspired by Perot to writer Todd Mason: "If Ross asked me to drive to

Alaska but he couldn't tell me why until I got there, I would be in my car an hour later."

It was that unblinking devotion, which stemmed from elusive, unnamable, but powerful qualities, that drove EDS during its lean years from 1962 until 1965. It was what Mort Meyerson said about Ross, how he was able to summon up untapped ardor from reluctant subordinates at a crucial moment by the push or pull of pride. "He was critical of my performance when things weren't going well," recalled Meyerson. "And he was full of praise when things did go well. And so I always knew where I stood. With Ross, you don't have to guess. That's a powerful thing, a very important characteristic—it's something rare in most human beings, much less management."

And the stories of Perot's iron will and sudden generosity were passed in whispers and warnings from ear to ear until they grew into legends. There was the parable of Tom Marquez, the third man hired by Ross Perot when he founded EDS in 1962. During the most crucial stage of the meetings in which Perot landed the all-important Frito-Lay account in 1963, the company's first multimillion-dollar deal, Tom's wife went into labor. Entangled in the high-level negotiations, Tom refused to leave the room at such a make-or-break stage. That is, he stayed until Perot threatened to fire him unless he left to attend to his wife at the hospital. The potato-chip deal went through without Marquez, but Perot became convinced that the child, a boy, was such a good-luck charm that T. J. Marquez eventually followed his father into the Perot company.

Such sagas bound employees to Perot on a much higher level than the typical straightforward relationship between labor and management. He was father and priest, leader and sometimes holy dispenser of wrath. Those who didn't cut their morality to suit his style were fired. He issued a formal decree: You could not discuss salary, you could not abuse drugs, you could not insult another human being, you could not tell lies, you must deal honorably with competitors and customers in the marketplace. Men would wear suits, and women would not wear slacks unless they had written permission. Divorce was not grounds for dismissal, but it did not help a career.

"It was never about a dress code or behavior," he says today. "It was about the practical matter of doing business."

"What is an EDSer?" he has asked rhetorically. "An EDSer is a person that goes anywhere, anytime, twenty-four hours a day, seven days a week, to make sure that EDS is the finest computer company in the world."

Though he could inspire his own troops with such simple, pious guidelines, he still had to pull in business. There were a few contracts that paid the rent, met the payroll, kept hope alive, but EDS was not the rocket that Ross Perot had first imagined. The federal Office of Economic Opportunity (OEO) gave him $250,000 to develop its computer system, but that ended after a year, and governmental prospects did not immediately improve. By 1965, Perot actually owned some major hardware—an IBM 360—but it wasn't large enough to handle the workload, and the gypsy programmers were still blown like pods across the Texas landscape at dusk.

Meanwhile, Perot was groping his way toward sophisticated management tactics, all within the boundaries of what he regarded as fair. He knew that he could get away with shamelessly prodding IBM, stealing its accounts as well as raiding its staff. He understood that its bureaucracy had grown flabby and slow to react. "One reason we could compete effectively with IBM is because we knew them so well," Gunn, the former IBM engineer, told Mason. "They were like a dinosaur. You could jab them in one place and they wouldn't feel it for a long time."

At one point, realizing that it was under some sort of assault from the pipsqueak company, IBM tried to withhold an essential software program from EDS, although it was the custom at the time to give away the software. Perot wrote a torrid letter to IBM headquarters, and the people at home office —sensitive to charges of monopolizing the industry and antitrust violations—ordered the Dallas branch to turn the software over to Perot. Little did they realize that they were handing him a gun.

Like all adversity, the slings and arrows endured by the EDSers pulled everyone together. Nevertheless, their boss was a puzzle. On the one hand, he had expressed populist beliefs in the wisdom and weight of the common man's opinion. On the other hand, once he had made up his mind on any given subject, he exerted his will. His was the last word, though he insists he operates on a cooperative basis.

Here was an executive inclined to turn over assignments to inexperienced people in whom he placed wild trust, leaving them without close supervision. But here was an executive who, if there was a problem, would appear out of nowhere and settle it like a hammer. Such a ubiquitous display of gifts drew his employees into tight circles of appreciation or hate. It also formed a hard, suspicious shell of resistance to the outside world. They later called themselves the Wild Bunch after the virtuous band of suicidal killers in the Sam Peckinpah movie. Some people referred to them as "warrior saints" working for the "Dallas Crusader." There were other appellations that still strike the EDSers as disgraceful and unfair—some detractors called Perot's dogged engineers and blitzkrieg salesmen the "Southern fascists."

There is a plaque outside the office of Ross Perot that is meant to both inspire and frighten those who seek his audience:

EVERY GOOD AND EXCELLENT THING STANDS MOMENT TO MOMENT ON THE RAZOR'S EDGE OF DANGER AND MUST BE FOUGHT FOR.

It is not so much a mantra as a warning: He is playing for very big stakes, and he knows it. If you want to put "some skin in the game," as he terms the ante for those who play at his table, you'd better be prepared to get skinned.

He understood from the first that it was going to take every bit of effort and attention to succeed.

And so he never put out less. Perot was always trying to improve his operation, always looking for
weaknesses or strengths. The boys would take lunch
at a quick barbecue stand every day, and Ross, who
never wasted time, even during a meal, was there
with them, eating the chicken, but measuring his
staff, testing the economic climate, and like a worried father with a delicate child, calculating the
company's life expectancy. Here was leadership,
here was ironclad control. Like it or be frightened
by the implications, nothing passed unnoticed,
nothing was wasted, nothing unexpected.

Nothing was unanticipated either, except, perhaps,
the bolt of luck that came down like thunder and
ultimately made Ross Perot as rich as Rockefellers
and Fords and all the kings of Babylon.

The pivotal event that catapulted EDS above the
economic clouds was the Great Society program.
Lyndon Johnson, a native son of Texas who had
gone on to become a master of congressional politics, then president of the United States after John
F. Kennedy was assassinated (ironically, in Dallas),
presented a great, sweeping agenda to wipe out pov-
erty, crushing medical costs, and social injustice. In
1965—as a tribute to Kennedy as much as a civic

duty—Congress enacted the Medicaid and Medicare bills.

It was a propitious moment in American politics. Government reacted to the sobering fact that adult children were going broke over the health costs of caring for their parents, and that senior citizens, in their twilight, were being impoverished by the skyrocketing cost of up-to-date medical care. Medical advances were stunning, but no one counted on the geometric rise in paying for all this technology. Medication alone cost a ransom. Sophisticated tests were only for the rich. People might live longer, but they couldn't afford to stay alive. Inevitably, people went untreated, suffered or died.

Under Medicare, the federal government would provide massive subsidies to the states so that they could safeguard the income of those over sixty-five. Under Medicaid, the government would attend to the medical needs of the indigent, those dependent upon welfare, the "categorically needy."

The complication was that nobody knew that the need was as vast and extensive as it turned out to be. These new entitlements affected one in every six Americans. State agencies administered the program; however, the Social Security Administration had oversight responsibility. It found state agencies swamped by the backlog of claims. No one seemed capable of coping with the paperwork, much less the demand for neglected medical care. The systems were in anarchic paralysis.

Enter Ross Perot. He had a running contract with the giant health insurer Blue Shield of Texas and understood the ins and outs of processing medical claims. He had long thought that the process needed modernizing, that computers were the answer to the trickle of claims that, under the benign prod of Medicaid, were bound to become a river in full flood.

Observers from all over the country flooded into Dallas and tried to study the system EDS had developed. Fraudulent claims were reduced, applicants found their checks in their mailboxes on time, and a great social program suddenly seemed capable of functioning efficiently. But Perot, as if he were protecting a precious patent—like his hero Thomas Edison—kept his software in the bowels of a closely guarded basement war room. (He would even shield it from his governmental benefactor, the Social Security Administration, which wanted to copy the software and use it elsewhere, claiming that its $250,000 in seed money was responsible for the programs in the first place; Perot took the administration to court and demonstrated that the $250,000 was a small percentage of the real cost of developing the system, which he claimed as his own. His argument was upheld.)

So extreme was Perot's security consciousness that he refused to publish a list of employees for fear that another firm would raid them, he refused to identify his customers for fear that they would be hounded for information about the system he used, and he won a battle with federal bureaucrats over limiting government access to his books.

Now that the industry saw what he could do, Perot was out on the road, selling EDS as if it were a new wonder drug that could cure the benefits-claims blahs. Within a year, he'd gotten contracts for running Medicaid billing operations in eleven states. "That was the breakthrough," he says. "Our only problem was controlling the growth of our business."

To Perot, it is an annoying and persistent source of recrimination and bitterness—to say nothing of high irony—that his riches came out of government programs to help the needy; one magazine in the early seventies even dubbed him the "Welfare Billionaire." There is simply no escaping the vivid (and valid) irony of a man who ended up in the lap of luxury by facilitating the dispensing of alms to the poor. But in a fair and open light, what he did can be viewed in another way. It can be seen as a simple twist of his early ambition to become an inventor. Perot's staff invented an efficient computer program to "move the goods" (process claims and payments) that outperformed all the other sloppy and lumbering competitors. In some cases, he won contracts through competitive bidding. In others, there simply was no realistic competition.

But there were cases in which Perot's cunning style cut through the opposition like a torch. Sometimes he could be high-handed and tough as nails and as crafty as a night stalker. For example, when he wanted to land the account to develop the computer program for Blue Shield, Perot turned to acquaintances who happened to be connected to "the Blues." It was the way—the only way—things were done, a backyard kind of thing left over from the Western traditions of hospitality. A man dropped into your camp, and you shared the beans and coffee. It was plain sociable, and, as they said, one hand washed the other.

One of these acquaintances—and a director of Texas Blue Shield at the time of the Great Society explosion—was James Aston, who also happened to be the chief operating officer of Dallas's largest bank, the Republic National Bank of Dallas. After being sold by Perot, Aston helped persuade other members of the board of Blue Shield to grant Perot the Blue Shield contract.

Later, when the dust settled, Aston the bank chairman became the chairman of Texas Blue Shield, and Perot became a director at the bank. There was a low-level congressional investigation, but nothing irregular, or illegal, was found, because nothing irregular or illegal was done; when reached recently, Aston declined to comment. No law was broken, no code violated. The only thing damaged was the tender sensibilities of those "politically correct" fanatics who saw in every business venture an industrial act of depravity. It might seem, in the glare of the new political hypersensitivity, something akin to a "sweetheart deal" to do business with neighbor or acquaintance, to grant contracts to someone you know, but in some cases businessmen, taxpayers, and consumers win. Perot knew the territory, he knew the product, he understood the game. EDS was the best choice.

There were some officials in the Social Security Administration who questioned the propriety of handing a contract to Perot without tough competitive bidding—even when there was no one able to compete. Walker Evans, then working as a local SSA official, told *New York Newsday* that he was "shocked" at the generous terms of the unprecedented three-year contract granted to Perot. According to his experts, claims should have cost thirty-six cents each. EDS charged $1.06, and profits may have been as high as 50 percent.

According to Meyerson, the EDS bid was unfairly computed. EDS provided ten times the computer power, compared to competing firms. Furthermore, other transactions cost $4 per claim, while EDS charged only $3. So while the profit ratio was higher, there was a net savings for the consumer.

Perot's argument against such criticism is that no one could bring in a claim at thirty-six cents. That was just bureaucratic skylarking, inventing numbers, impractical. His profit margins were, Mort Meyerson insists, a genuine bargain, considering that the job was handled cleanly and without messy aftershocks.

"It was a fair price," Meyerson says. "No one else could have done it."

By 1968, EDS employed 323 full-time workers, had assets of about $10 million, and was pulling in profits of more than $1.5 million annually. The number of state Medicare contracts was now twenty-three, the growth curve was dizzyingly upward, and it was then that there arose a real temptation for a quick financial killing. It was being dangled like a ripe fruit in front of Perot's eyes by squads of investment bankers who sensed mouth-watering possibilities in such a stock offering. The stock market was in a feeding frenzy at the time. All Perot would have to do would be to take the company public—allow shares to be sold on the Big Board of the Stock Exchange in New York—and his holdings would guarantee his lasting wealth. He was not yet a rich man. Ross Perot's salary remained at $68,000 annually throughout the seventies and eighties, but he held the bulk of the shares in EDS, and he was, only from a theoretical point of view, a millionaire.

Perot was reluctant to let go of any large part of his company, even if he would maintain ultimate control. Investment bankers laid out the strategies of the deal, the likely outcome, the possible profits. But still Perot balked. The Stock Exchange was not something familiar, not something knowable. Men made millions on something as insubstantial as a hunch, and it bothered him. There was that old fear of the great crash of '29. The Depression was a remembered event in his life. Those hoboes coming to his back door in Texarkana were, in a large measure, blown there by the gusts of that crash. The market bent and broke in winds he did not feel or touch or even understand.

"Ross does not like to get into something in which, even when you do everything right, you can still fail," says Margot of her husband's business instincts. "He had that same reaction when someone wanted to sell him a resort in Vail, Colorado. He thought about it, and it looked good, but then he shook his head and said no. It was that same thing. You could do everything just right, but because it didn't snow or it didn't rain—in the case of a farmer, he has said that they can work their hearts out and do everything right, and then lose it all. He probably did get that from the cotton."

There was no shortage of suitors. The underwriters who sell the stock had done their research and knew that there was heat in this well-run, closely held high-tech company. During the spring and summer of 1968, one by one, they came down to Dallas and made their pitch, but Perot, as if adhering to some keener sense of timing, was in no hurry. He was unimpressed by the parade, until he encountered Ken Langone, who was representing the blue-chip firm of R. W. Pressprich and Company, but still had in his voice the authentic sound of an Italian-American street urchin from the Bronx.

"There was great affinity," recalls Langone.

What happened on the first meeting was a quick and lasting friendship. There was an immediate stripping away of pretense. These two men both had solid roots in family and great self-confidence in their own hard climb to success. The trust between them was instantaneous. They were both "winners," and prided themselves that they did it by adhering to the rules of the game.

"I will tell you a remarkable thing about this deal," says Langone. "Ross Perot sent a memo to all his employees. It was about the value of doing the right thing as a public company. You had to do your job and do it well and do it low-key. The company would frown upon any promotional activity, any projections. The slightest hint of impropriety in the way of tipping people off as to what was going on would not be tolerated. I think of this now, because this is before Mike Milken and all the insider activity. There was nothing 'insider' about Ross Perot. It was all out front."

Langone brought with him to Dallas a battery of lawyers to put together a complicated public offering. "The impression Ross had of Easterners was that they all went to Ivy League schools, they all wore brown wing tips—or alligator shoes," Langone remembers. "And they all had Locust Valley lockjaw accents. Well, one day, we're working on a document, and at noon, he says, 'Let's go to lunch.'

"He takes us to this dive, Johnny Cummings' Barbecue Pit. And we go down there, and obviously Perot has prearranged this, the guy who owns the place has a filthy rag and he wipes the top of the counter. We've got cafeteria trays, and some of these lawyers, who were from fine old Wall Street firms, and who did speak in this proper Ivy League accent, were aghast. Their faces were pale with worry over this meal. The guy behind the counter says, 'What'll you have?' and the lawyers asked apprehensively, 'What do you suggest?' So Johnny Cummings says, 'You oughta try that barbecued armadillo, it's real good.' Now these lawyers are figuring they can't afford to offend Perot—this is his place—and they take the 'armadillo,' which was probably pork, to the table, and Perot's sitting there, and he's watching. There are five of us pushing the food around the plate and trying not to eat it, and Ross is having a great time."

The day the deal went through—September 12,

1968—Langone got his revenge. Ross was in New York at the company headquarters at 80 Pine Street, and after he signed the papers, he thought he was being taken by Langone to a fancy Wall Street haunt for lunch.

"What's the name of it?" Ross asked.

"It's called the Umbrella Club," Langone replied. "It's so exclusive very few people know about it. I've got the limousine down in the garage."

Langone had brought in a picnic table to the basement of the company headquarters. He paid a street vendor twenty-five dollars to wheel in a standard-issue, New York City–type hot-dog cart to the basement. Perot laughed and ate his hot dog and accepted, as he usually does, the table being turned on his joke.

Perot didn't just go public—he brought everyone concerned in on the deal (not unlike his global two-way television town-meeting concept for governing the nation.) The employees' shares were to be split ten for one, and he organized a company meeting to discuss the ramifications. Everyone was allowed to come to the microphone and speak his or her piece. When the level of enthusiasm at the meeting built too high, Perot assumed a devil's advocate role and pointed out the pitfalls. The stock could collapse. They could all wind up with worthless paper.

But in the end, the deal went through. Underwriters purchased 650,000 shares, which represented only 6 percent of the company's outstanding 11.5 million shares. Perot himself held 9.5 million shares. On that first day, EDS stock opened at $16.50 a share, then climbed to $23 by the closing bell. Within a year, it was selling for $160 a share and would eventually increase to $200, making Perot worth almost $2 billion. By age thirty-eight, he had become a billionaire. *Fortune* magazine called him "The Fastest, Richest Texan Ever."

Langone saw the article in *Fortune* and called Ross to congratulate him. The next day, Margot phoned Langone at home. She told him how Ross was handling his new celebrity. "There had been a lot of publicity at the time about Jackie Kennedy marrying Aristotle Onassis," Langone recalls. "And Margot said that Ross was looking from the story about himself to another one about Jackie, and he was being very contemplative. Finally, she turned to him and said, 'Ross, what are you thinking about?' He said, 'Oh, I was just thinking, if Jackie waited a few more months, she might've made a different decision.'"

9

"I was right—it was never boring."

—MARGOT PEROT

Ross Perot seemed to be sprinting in a world stuck in the mud of too many managers and too many controls. At times he overwhelmed people with his blunt approach and high energy and his unpredictable impulses.

And yet the balances of his life swung delicately like the pendulum of some finely tuned clock, shifting between solid, rational conduct and moments of reckless, immoderate adventure. He was a big businessman spinning deals to the world by day, then became a playful, adoring father to his five children at the dinner table. Always, he was an intrepid husband and understanding friend to his wife.

More than anyone, Margot recognized that he was also percolating with something unsettled, something more dangerous and explosive than anyone else in their safe, predictable world. If he had undomesticated whims, the truth was, Margot had them, too. If he had no patience for small worries, or timidity, and he had no time for half measures, she managed to keep up with his views and agree with his agenda. He lived his life on a bungee cord of daredevil antics, and Margot was there, with him, more than a mere spectator. The truth was that she was having a great time. "I've supported him from the very beginning because he can solve problems better than anyone I've ever seen," she says. "No matter what the situation. He could always sift right through to the heart of the matter. Just don't think of too many things at once, he'd always say. Just take it one piece at a time."

She remembers a day in winter when Ross woke up full of vinegar and fire, as he was on most days, and said, in that casual way he has when he is about to leap off into space, "Let's go for a ride." They were at their lake house on Lake Texoma, and she knew that he meant that he wanted to go for a sprint around the water on the boat. Not just the cabin cruiser, but the cigarette boat. The knifelike speedboat designed to break speed records or demonstrate pluck on the water. She was putting on a ski mask because she knew how hard the wind blew when the cigarette boat got up to speed on the lake, sometimes skimming across the water at 80 miles an hour, when she thought, Hold it, wait a minute, this is crazy! Then she smiled and slipped the hood over her face, because the truth was that she liked the sense of speed and the feel of the wind smacking her hard, putting color and maybe a little of his fire into her own face, and she went ahead, in the dead of winter, because she had signed on for the full ride.

"He just likes the adventure," she says. "He says he doesn't, but he does. At Vail, they groom the slopes at night so that they're nice and smooth for the skiers. And it's so glorious when you go down these long, snowy trails. And every now and then we'll be crossing something, we'll be going over these big bumps, and he'll say, 'Now, if I wanted pain, I would go over Niagara Falls in a barrel.'"

But he was pursuing something risky down the slopes at Vail. There was that impetuous part of his nature that stood unflinching against . . . something. He'd had a scrappy, aggressive, confrontational, and unyielding outlook on life since childhood. Since he first heard the cowboy legends. Since he first listened to a voice on the radio half a world away uttering defiance in the face of disaster. It seeped into an everyday stance. His personal hero remains Winston Churchill, and at every opportunity he recites Churchill's credo, which he's made his own as well: "Never give in. Never give in. Never! Never! Never!"

It was a consistent and unswerving theme in his life: Ross Perot rescued lost cats, ailing children, wounded spouses, tapped-out workers; he tried to rescue prisoners, hostages, maverick cops, the New York City mounted-police unit, a museum for American Indians, Wall Street, the nation—even a copy of the Magna Carta. It often seemed that he only had to hear a sad tale of woe or the bugle call of his Boy Scout youth and he was on his white horse, plunging forth. Sometimes it worked, and sometimes he was Don Quixote, tilting at windmills.

And so, because his shield was not confined to friends, family, and employees, when Henry Kissinger called from the White House in late 1969 and said that American prisoners in Vietnam were suffering, and the government could not act because it would be a sign of weakness, Ross Perot didn't hesitate.

It was a time when President Richard Nixon, newly elected by the thinnest of margins, was under pressure from antiwar demonstrators and didn't want to add fuel to the turmoil. Some sort of emotional counterweight was seen by the White House as necessary to divert attention from the protestors. And Perot, counted by the Nixon administration as a true friend, was the answer.

Perot went to Washington. He talked about his meeting with Henry Kissinger years later to *The Washington Post*. He quoted Kissinger, who had brought him to his White House office: "Ross, our intelligence reports say that half the POWs in Vietnam will die of brutality or neglect before the war is over. We have to do something about it, but we can't do it ourselves. Can you help us?" Perot cleared his mission with Alexander Haig, who was then Kissinger's deputy.

"We knew he was passionate about what was happening to the boys," Haig told the *Post*. "We knew he had something to offer more than just money."

While not confirming every detail, Haig does give Perot's version great credence. "I would not say we formally asked him to do it as such," he told *The New York Times* in 1992, "but we endorsed the concept. There were a number of things that Ross conceived of, including ransoming the prisoners with his own capital. I think the fellow put his money where his mouth was and I have nothing but the highest admiration for him."

One thing that he had, beyond money, was purity of heart. He would act as a private citizen, he told the White House bravely. He would bring to the issue the kind of publicity that would ensure that the POWs were treated fairly. How would he do that? He decided to pay a Christmas visit to Hanoi. He would bring two planeloads of gifts and mail—and journalists. The whole world would be watching.

"He wanted to get big planes," recalls Ken Langone, who had become Perot's friend and confidant since their Wall Street episode. The only plane they had was a long-range version of the 707. Well, he needed two long-range planes, and he asked me if I could make some calls to the airlines to see if we could charter a couple of planes."

Langone shakes his head.

"So, I just went nuts. This is late '69, Christmas. The airlines were all busy. I said, 'Ross, I don't know what the hell we're going to do, I can't get the planes.' There was a pause. Then he said to me, 'Well, aren't these guys all in bad shape, financially?'

"I said, 'Yeah.'

"Then he said, 'Why don't we just go and buy two?' "

Langone started laughing. He had still not adjusted to the swooping style of his friend from Texas. "He said, 'What's so funny?'

"I said, 'You know, there's only one thing worse than nouveau rich,' I said, 'that's nouveau *very* rich.' "

Ross laughed, because he could laugh at himself, but, significantly, he kept after the planes anyway. Eventually, he leased them.

There were reasons for his passion. There was that strain of strong native patriotism. One look at his office, with its sacred, secular relics (including busts of Lincoln and Teddy Roosevelt, inspirational messages, original Norman Rockwell paintings, a Gilbert Stuart portrait of George Washington, the Remington bronze castings of cowboys, the carvings of eagles, battle-torn flags, and pictures of the soldiers and sailors he has helped, along with the thank-you letters), leaves no doubt about the reach of his emotions, or the exact nature of his allegiance. America is pure gospel to him. In addition, a lot of the employees at EDS were ex-servicemen. They were recruited at Camp Lejeune and Fort Hood and had a military esprit de corps. All knew (or had friends who knew) someone lost in the jungles of Southeast Asia. And Perot himself had more than a few Annapolis classmates in Vietnamese POW camps. He had been thirsting to do something bold about it.

Personal connections aside, the truth was that, at the time, Nixon picked Perot because he was doggedly anticommunist and was undeniably identified with the political right wing; the Nixon administration was frustrated by the left's cornering sentiment to free the POWs by simply ending the war.

He had long since come to the simple conclusion that the opinion of the world played a big role in the behavior of the North Vietnamese. He decided to beat them at their own game.

To win back the hearts and minds of the world, he flew 150 relatives of Vietnam POWs to Paris to linger in the background of the young peace talks, where they would remain a haunting presence. They held press conferences and protested Hanoi's failure to adhere to the Geneva Convention provision on treatment of prisoners. Perot claims that it raised the thermostat of world sympathy toward improving the treatment of the POWs.

Meanwhile (in keeping with his philosophy of a multitrack attack on problems, so that if one fails another can succeed), he loaded two Boeing stretch 707s with gifts, food, medicine, and journalists. The money didn't matter, but in this instance, the publicity did.

"He didn't want to draw attention to himself," recalls Margot of that first trip. "But he understood that was the only way to draw attention to the plight of the prisoners of war."

Up until then, the State Department had been urging the families of the POWs to play down the problem. "They told the wives and mothers, 'The less said the better; just don't ripple the waters,'" Perot recalls. "They'd been saying that for so long that we decided that the best way to handle it was just the opposite. Say something. Ripple the waters."

Ross tried to clear his trip through diplomatic channels, but the North Vietnamese kept throwing up roadblocks. Another obstacle came on his way to Anchorage when word came that the North Vietnamese had put up another condition: They would not accept big packages. Everything had to be wrapped in small packages, nine by twelve.

When Perot landed in Alaska, the hangar was crowded with volunteers who had heard about the new condition attached to the mission.

"From all over the city, they came to the hangar, and they took this huge cargo and repacked it," recalls Margot. "They worked all through the night and got them repacked, and he started out again in the morning."

As they came closer to Hanoi, the North Vietnamese became tougher. "They said, 'No, we can't take the packages, but you can deliver them to Moscow,'" Perot recalls.

Moscow agreed to accept the medicine and food and mail, but it was a ragged trip because other communist countries refused Perot's planes permission to fly in its airspace to reach the Soviet capital.

"Every time they would close a door, he would find a way to reopen it," says Margot. "Over Denmark, Ross called the Russian embassy there from the plane, got someone at home, who told him, 'Don't you know that we never have done this before, we would never give you permission in the first place?'

"And Ross said, 'Well, I probably did know that, but I wanted the world to know that you were refusing this humanitarian gesture.'"

10

"You're gonna get skinned out there."

—A ROSS PEROT PEP TALK

When Perot attempted his Christmas visit to Vietnam, his two red-and-green Braniff 707s had been denied landing rights. They had bounced around the sky from one denied airspace to another. He was ridiculed in the press and in a private whispering campaign of deniability. The State Department, attempting to put some distance between the government and this gallant but futile gesture, made this condescending comment:

"We look on him as a rich but eccentric uncle," said a spokesman. "One may secretly admire his eccentricity, but one doesn't want to get too close for fear of what he may do next."

There were reports of secret offers to ransom prisoners from the North Vietnamese for $100 million, but Perot steadfastly has denied them. Still, Wall Street got jittery over a loose canon loaded with a couple of billion dollars. In one day in the winter of 1970, the value of his stock declined by $450 million. It was the single greatest loss by an individual in the history of the stock exchange. Yet Perot shrugged it off. "I'd be more upset if one of my kids broke a finger," he said.

But his pride was wounded, and he didn't intend to let the matter lie there. In March of 1970, he began contacting reporters, as well as rounding up another planeload of gifts for the POWs. He was going to try to go to Hanoi again.

Hugh McDiarmid, then a columnist for the *Dayton Journal-Herald*, was one of the invited journalists. "Few of us knew much about Perot except that he was successful in business," he wrote in 1992. "I recall this exchange, amid the anticommunist incantations and mission statements presented at the departure briefing in Dallas:

"Reporter: 'Mr. Perot, do you want us to call you a "millionaire" or a "billionaire"?'

"Perot: 'Just call me Ross.' "

According to McDiarmid, Perot was again humiliated, again spurned by the North Vietnamese, even when he took a side trip to Vientiane, Laos, where, accompanied by POW wives, he stood outside the North Vietnamese embassy and pleaded through a loudspeaker for better treatment for the POWs. It sounds a little foolish, as described by McDiarmid, with the wives and reporters made to wait in a steaming shed for seven hours, then Perot banging ineffectually on a locked gate at the embassy before flying off to the next stop on his crusade. But there is something infinitely moving about a man of such wealth and power making himself so vulnerable for the sake of American prisoners.

It was not all futile. In spite of the ridicule and the distance placed between the administration and Perot's attempt to help the hostages, there are letters and testimonials proclaiming that conditions did, indeed, improve after Perot's trips. And Perot points to further proof. He has a 1974 proclamation signed by then-defense secretary James R. Schlesinger, awarding him the Defense Department's Medal for Distinguished Public Service. It was given for his work on behalf of the prisoners of war.

In that same year, Perot wanted to share his experiences with his family. So he decided on a round-the-world trip. Ross and Margot took their son, Ross junior, then thirteen, as well as daughter

Nancy, then ten, and flew to Hawaii and Japan and then into Vientiane when the Vietnam War was still raging. "As we flew into Laos, we could look down and see people fighting on the ground," recalls Ross.

Nancy stayed in Hong Kong with Margot while Ross and his son spent three days on the aircraft carrier *Enterprise* as it sailed in the South China Sea and conducted air operations in Vietnam. There are pictures of the father and son on the bridge wearing the baseball caps of the fleet. Ross junior watched the pilots take off and land. "He couldn't get over how young they were," says Perot. "See, he thought of pilots as airline pilots. He thought they'd be much older men. But these were kids going off that flight deck.

"They'd let him stand back with the landing signal officer as the planes came back from missions. They were all shot up; rockets that never fired were hanging by the wires. They'd hit that restraining net, and things would start flying all over the flight deck. I mean, it was chaos central."

The young fliers came back from their missions soaked in sweat, and sometimes blood, and young Ross and old Ross were awed by what they were witnessing.

Recalls the father, "And I'll never forget, he walked up to one of the young pilots who was climbing out of his airplane, and he says, 'Boy, it must really be hot in that cockpit.' The guy was covered with sweat. And this young guy—in his early twenties—looked at him and said, 'I'm not sweating 'cause it was hot.'"

Ross junior knows what he saw. He remembers standing on the bridge watching the pilots take off. "Met the pilots before the missions," he says. "Met pilots and two hours later they'd been shot down and killed." Later, Ross junior, no doubt intoxicated by the drama of that rare youthful glimpse into the glory and gore of battle, would become an air-force fighter pilot.

On that same trip around the world, they stopped in Israel and were afforded access to all the powers that be. It was only a few years after the Six-Day War, and everyone was still overwhelmed by the Israeli victory. The Perots were briefed by no less a figure than General Ariel Sharon. He began describing a battle but was interrupted by Ross junior, who knew some tactics and wanted more detail. As the father describes with pride, "General Sharon stopped talking to me. For about thirty minutes, he talked to Ross junior, man to man, and explained the battle.

"Now Sharon's a tough guy, right? But here's this little boy who was obviously fascinated."

They were given an audience with the head of the Israeli Air Force, then ushered into a secret sanctum where they met a venerable gray-haired woman. It was Golda Meir, the prime minister. "Someone must have told her who I was—she wouldn't know me—and she was smart and wise and very nice," recalls Ross of the visit. "I can't even remember what she said, but it was impressive."

There was a meeting with Teddy Kollek, the mayor of Jerusalem, who took them around and showed them the Old City and the spirit of light and hope for peace that had not yet been dimmed by the Palestinian rebellion and Israeli intransigence.

"Now that's a wonderful experience for a child to have."

They are all fair and even-tempered, moderated by the sunny disposition of their mother. They smile easily—lucky children born into a happy home.

Each, in his or her own way, is tongue-tied with

gratitude over the fact that they are who they are. And they are, after all, a prince and four princesses.

Ross junior, of course, was the charmed one, the son, the firstborn, the heir, but if there is feminist resentment among his four younger sisters, it's not apparent. They accepted his succession; they all recognized the mystical bond—not that they had much choice. Between these two, father and son, there was an implicit understanding of the torch being passed, of posterity—an acknowledged patrimony—that stretched back for generations; it glanced over an electric emotion that neither of them could name, but both acknowledged. Here was the grandchild who never met his revered dead grandfather but who carried his genes, as well as every other parcel in that weighty legacy. Looked at in a certain light and in a certain way, Ross junior resembled his grandfather Gabriel. And, finally, in Ross junior, Ross found some consolation for the loss of his own father.

Ross junior was born in 1958. He had some of his father's tenacity; you could see it in his earnest, solemn expression. But it lacked lethal fire. He could dig in and get stubborn just like his old man, but you could also see that it took effort and wasn't natural. He inherited more of his mother's easygoing manner as well as her refined good looks. Maybe it was a fondness for food, which made him overly conscious of his waistline and slightly less intimidating. He was taller and broader than Ross; there was a familiar, crisp discipline in his comportment, and he called men "sir" and women "ma'am." But there was no soft-tissue scarring on his nose from falling off horses, no jug-eared antennae bracketing a burr haircut. He didn't come at you like an angry cactus plant. There was an endearing softness to the son that simply wasn't part of his father's makeup—but on the inside his parents found him tough as steel.

"I was born when he was still a computer salesman for IBM, so I basically watched the American dream unfold," Ross junior says. "He always included me anytime he could. Which is very important, for a young boy to watch his father."

When his father was struggling with EDS, Ross junior would spend Saturdays at the computer center. "This is back when they had punch cards, and I'd collect thousands of punch cards in my room at home. The computer operators would even print out Snoopy calendars for me."

He would, as a matter of pride, try to copy his father's capers. At the St. Mark's private school,

Ross junior rode his horse through the halls. "I got a couple of detentions for that."

He didn't get into too much trouble because this was Texas, and riding a horse through a school does not carry the same stigma as it would in, say, Manhattan. But the principal was "an East Coast guy, and he didn't understand about horses. He thought that if the horses got out of control they would hurt someone, so that's what I got in trouble for—poor judgment."

These were gentle horses, and there was one occasion when Ross rode into the faculty lounge and the horse rested his head gently on the shoulder of Ross's adviser, who had been reading a magazine. Unperturbed, the adviser said, "Ross, you really ought to get that horse out of here."

The punishments from his father were identical to the ones that Ross senior and Bette had suffered from Lulu May: the glare and the lecture.

After Ross junior came Nancy, who was born in 1960 and would eventually take business courses and become a driving force in her father's later career. She would handle new projects, tenderize the blows when Ross was brusque, and demonstrate an acute agility in the office atmosphere of hard-charging high achievers.

Suzanne was born in 1964 and had artistic inclinations. She went off to New York with her husband and made a career in an art auction house. Then came Carolyn, born in 1968 and judged the closest of the brood to Ross. Once, when she was a child, and in a tough dispute with her father, Ross remembers her standing her ground and looking him in the eye, hands on hips, saying, "You know what the problem is, don't you? I'm just like you."

Last came Katherine, born in 1971, full of spit and light, the only one with her father's agate eyes and short fuse and bristling wit.

All told, the Perots were more than just a mother, father, and five children; they were, in the truest sense of the word, a family.

In 1990, Margot threw a party for Ross Perot at the Mansion on Turtle Creek, a lavish restaurant built and owned by one of the Perot family's few peers in the finance department, a member of the Hunt family. The dinner was held on June 27—Ross's sixtieth birthday—and he was presented with a gift. Over the years and with his expanding fortunes, he'd gotten many presents, but this one was different, overshadowing all the others: This was an album from his children. There were pictures of Ross as a child with his father, riding the Tennessee walkers in Texarkana. There were photos of him as a young midshipman, as a sailor, as a young suitor and groom. There were portraits of the children and the grandchildren. The album traced a straight line from that rough beginning when he was tossing newspapers on cathouse steps, to the private chopper pads, vacation homes, and white-water rafting trips of his maturity. And there, tucked between the pages of his well-documented triumph, were the sentimental snapshots of him dancing with Margot, their eyes lit by an undimmed fire.

But perhaps even more touching than the photographs were the tributes from the children, snippets and rhymes wrapped together like a bouquet, each handwritten and capturing some remembered essential truth about the relationships.

From Carolyn:

"I have many favorite memories, too many to list, but the biggest surprise of my life was when you and Mommy showed up at Camp Seafarer . . ."

Margot laughs. She remembers that summer when they surprised Carolyn. "She must've been more homesick than we realized," Margot says. "It was a surprise visit, and when she looked at him [Ross], she just ran up and wrapped her arms and legs around him."

"Another of many happy moments was when you gave me 'Honey' the cat. I begged and I begged to keep the newfound kitten. Finally, you led me to believe that I'd won a bet when I know you intended to let me keep her all along. That's the way you are. You love to make me feel smart and special. You've given me so much confidence, obviously too much, in myself. Also, I'll never forget the time you surprised me after 'Outward Bound.' You flew all the way to Maine, in between meetings in Washington, D.C., just to tell me how proud you were. I love you so much. You're the best. I don't get to tell you enough."

She signed it "Super Care." It was a nickname, just like the special private names he had for all the girls (Ross junior was always Ross). Nancy was "Little Nan," Suzanne was "BBD," which stood for "my beautiful blond daughter," and Katherine was "Special K."

From Katherine:

"My first memories of you are riding on King Cotton as you chanted silly songs to the beat of the hooves. . . . 'Sweet Kath-er-ine in her flying machine with her tail painted red and her nose painted green. . . .'"

The stories are presented like sunbursts in their past. The stables in front of the house are almost empty now, but Katherine remembers her riding lessons, when her gnarly old father put her up on "Tony-the-pony" and told her not to be afraid. Tony was a high-spirited horse, but if he bucks you off, Ross said, "get right back on and show him who's boss." And she repledged an old promise to "be like Grandmother, although I could never do such a fine woman justice, I'll do my best."

Of course the children were all pampered—they were the visible, glittering proof of the marital bliss. Ross and Margot, both in their separate ways, doted on the children, spoiled them, delighted in them, and took immense pride in the achievements and poise of their five offspring.

11

"Once you pay the bills, money is the most overrated thing in the world."

—ROSS PEROT

Now that he was rich—Texas rich, with piles of money bubbling with interest in the bank like an endless underground pool of oil—and had real assets beyond his relatively tiny $68,000 annual salary, Perot established a charitable foundation. He didn't do it for the tax break; in fact, for several years he refused to take a charitable tax deduction on the grounds that whatever wealth he had he owed to his country.

To administer his philanthropies through the Perot Foundation, Ross convinced his sister, Bette, to give up her job as an assistant principal in Fort Worth and move into his office complex. Her influence was felt. Not only was she a former teacher, but so was Margot, and Perot had a deep, unshakable belief in the curative powers of education. There were those who found it inconceivable when one of his first acts was to make a $2.4 million grant to the Dallas school system. The money was earmarked for a special learning program at one of the inner-city black elementary schools. The general opinion about him was that he was a thin-skinned, right-wing philistine. "From the day I first had money I've been trying to solve problems that a lot of liberals just wring their hands about," he told a reporter for *Texas Monthly*.

When the New York City Police Department's mounted unit was in danger of folding because of lack of money—something Suzanne read in the newspapers and pointed out to her father—he sent sixteen Tennessee walkers and saddles to keep the patrol alive. When the Museum of the American Indian in upper Manhattan sent a letter asking for assistance, he dispatched an aide, then offered the museum $70 million to relocate in Dallas, where he thought an Indian museum would be more fitting anyway.

New York municipal officials declined.

There has always been a high degree of oversight (or meddling, depending on your point of view) in the disbursement of Perot's gifts. He may believe in civic duty and in the rich tithing, but he also believes in getting substantive and significant value for his money. He drives, as many have noted, a hard bargain, even when the only thing at stake is pride.

When the North Texas Food Bank wanted to borrow money to rent a warehouse, Perot costed out the expense and decided it was cheaper to buy his own warehouse for $1.5 million and let the food bank use it rent-free. The difference is that the foundation controls it and can make certain it is used to serve the poor.

Bishop College in Dallas, an all-black school deeply in debt, also asked for a large donation, but Perot refused. His money would not have the same beneficial effect as the $2.4 million he gave to the well-run learning program in the primary grades, he said. He drove home the same lesson when he canceled an $8 million pledge to the Dallas Arboretum and Botanical Society, claiming that the expansion project was not meeting his standards for being "world class," and was mired in controversy. "I wanted them to build a park next to the arboretum, so that everyone would have a safe place to go with their families. They wanted to put it inside the arboretum—that's when I canceled the pledge."

Resisting efforts to donate money to the University of Texas's Southwestern Medical School in Dallas, Perot reportedly was unimpressed by the institution's reputation. "I've never read about it in *Time* magazine or *The New York Times*," he said. "I have no knowledge that it's a great medical school." This was in 1985. And six months later, on October 14, 1985, when two members of the Southwestern faculty—Dr. Joseph Goldstein and Dr. Michael Brown—won Nobel prizes in medicine, a fundraiser asked Perot, "What's your perception now?"

"This is going to cost me a lot of money," he replied. Perot eventually pledged $20 million over ten years to attract, according to Perot, "the next generation of Browns and Goldsteins."

This combination of zealous, hands-on management and supervision, in addition to his inability to turn away from a challenge framed in patriotic bunting, would cost Perot heavily at the start of the seventies, when he was rampant with confidence and at the height of public-spirited fervor.

During the early seventies, Perot was preoccupied with high-profile patriotism. It was the season of discontent over Vietnam, and the nation was alive with marches and countermarches, protesting and supporting the war. He was an old sailor, and he volunteered to join the army of the Silent Majority. In fact, he offered to sponsor a campaign to give voice to the Silent Majority. He had dinners with President Nixon, sailed down the Potomac on the presidential yacht *Sequoia*, was a guest at important public functions, and was counted as one of those with deep pockets and a reliable ideology. But in the end, he saw that he would be tossing money down the drain, and maybe even balked at the mismanagement of the war (although not the spirit behind it) and gently backed away from intimate identification with the lost cause of Richard Nixon.

Not that it soured the administration on Ross Perot.

One morning late in 1970, Ross Perot got another one of those breathless, flag-waving, the-country-needs-you bugle calls from the White House. First there was Attorney General John Mitchell on the line, then Treasury Secretary John Connally, then half a dozen White House aides, assistants, deputies, all with the same plea. Du Pont, Glore Forgan & Company, the nation's second-largest stock brokerage firm, was about to collapse, and the New

York Stock Exchange—wholesale consumers of the then-fashionable domino theory—reckoned that Du Pont could take the rest of the Street with it. This would cause a major panic, bringing down all other money markets, as well as Western civilization.

The first problem was cash. The family-run firm had been guilty of sloppy management, and the downturn of the market in 1969 and 1970 left it weak. Perot immediately transferred $10 million to Du Pont. "As long as there is a Wall Street, we will owe a tremendous debt of gratitude to Ross Perot," said an emotional Bernard J. (Bunny) Lasker, chairman of the New York Stock Exchange.

However, the Wall Street titans expected Perot to dip into his deep pockets but not interfere with traditional methods of operation. This was a fundamental misreading of Perot's character. He is a hands-on white knight.

"We'd been told by all sorts of people that the free market as we know it would disappear if we let Du Pont go under," recalls Meyerson. "But the truth is, the deeper we got into it, the worse it looked. I mean, it never got better, and it never settled down. We talked to some executives from the Street and asked them if they'd consider being CEO, and of course everybody turned it down.

Then, finally, Ross turned to me one day and said, 'Look, Mort, we have to do this. We've got the means to do it. If we lose it, we lose it. We can't get any executive to come and do this, so it looks like you'll have to move to New York and do it.' I said, 'Ross, how could you conceive of a plan like that?' And he said, 'We don't have any alternative.' So I moved to New York."

Meyerson was thirty-two at the time and imbued with old military, EDS high-performance expectations. That is, he marched into Wall Street like a combat command of Patton's Third Army, expecting soldiers to wear ties and polished helmets in battle. Instead, there was wholesale desertion under fire. The freewheeling brokers were unwilling to bend to what they regarded as an authoritarian regime. The climate was definitely unfriendly to this upstart outsider (Perot) and his hired gun (Meyerson).

"Now that was tough pressure," Meyerson recalled. "That was going in. And going in there were stories that we did it for altruistic reasons, there were stories that we really wanted to make a fortune, and there were stories that we really wanted to reform Wall Street.

"Well, we made money the first year, we lost a

little bit of money the second year, we lost some money the third year. And then the Arab oil embargo hit, and I knew instantaneously that the market was going to be terrible for the foreseeable future.

"So in March of 1974, I went to Ross and said, 'We either have got to put up more money and stay the course, and if we do that, we'll make a lot of money back—I think we'll make five to ten times our investment after the markets get good again—but we've got to bridge this gap, this Grand Canyon.'

"And he said, 'No, I'd rather stop it.'

"I said, 'We're going to have to do it quickly, because we don't want any customers hurt, and I don't want to take Chapter Eleven.'

"He said, 'I agree; we shouldn't take Chapter Eleven. Just do it quickly and surgically. Do the best you can.'

"Now this is a man who stood to lose fifty or sixty million dollars, and he was very cool about it. Actually, there was some tension between us at the time because Ross was not happy with the performance of Du Pont. I wasn't happy with the performance of Du Pont! He was in Texas. I was in New York. This wasn't the happiest time for either one of us. And yet, in a flash, when put to the test, he said, 'Look, you just have to do the right thing. Go do it.' And I did. I spent the next year extricating ourselves from that situation."

There was some bitterness about the resistance he received from the traditional Wall Street establishment. "They oughta put a red light outside that place," Perot said.

"They wanted to take him down a peg," Ken Langone told *The New York Times*. "He was a newly rich Texan. They were happy to see him go down, even if Du Pont's survival would have helped them in the long run."

Again, Meyerson was impressed by how Ross Perot handled losing. "When people get defeated, they get mean and nasty, and they get vindictive," he says. "They start looking for scapegoats. Ways out. He could easily have come up with a plan to save as much money as you can for himself and to hell with the customers. We don't have any obligation to them anyway. Not really. Chapter Eleven is legal. It's a shield. It never occurred to him."

To close the brokerage, Perot brought in a young Dallas lawyer, Tom Luce. "I went to his office and met with him, and he said that he had made up his mind to shut down the brokerage firm," Luce recalls. "He said, 'If you had a hardware store in Texarkana and you weren't making money, you'd just close it down. You'd settle up with everybody and just close it down. That's what I want to do.'

"What made it amazing was that I was a thirty-four-year-old lawyer who had just opened an office, and he was asking me to liquidate the second-largest brokerage firm in the nation," continues Luce. "He was interviewing major law firms in Washington, D.C., and in New York, and most businessmen would've done the conservative thing, hired a known commodity. But he took a chance. I said that I'd drop everything else to work on it, and I know that impressed him."

It wasn't quite so simple. Luce found that he would receive twenty-five or thirty phone calls a day from Perot asking laserlike questions about details, progress, pitfalls, when he was working on a project. And when he went on his bicycle rides, he'd come back with questions. Have you thought of X or Y?

"Those of us close to Ross do not anxiously await the end of his bicycle rides," says Luce.

Meyerson has a theory that explains why Ross Perot is unique among the superrich. "One of the things that Ross has in his favor is that he became so wealthy and so powerful and so well known so fast that he never had to prove himself to anyone," he says. "He never had to prove anything to anybody."

Most people who come into great wealth in their own lifetime, through the sweat of their brow, make concessions, bend to others who are more powerful, grow corrupt. But Perot's wealth was so sudden that he never went through that smelting process. His ethical core remained intact.

"And he never worried about dignity," Meyerson says. "I guess if you're that self-confident, in the most profound way, you don't have to worry about dignity because it exists."

Of course Perot was tough and demanding. "Once he gets on your back, he can stay on your back," Meyerson says. "One time, in 1976, I was working on a contract in California that was going to be the best contract in the history of EDS. I had come back to EDS from Wall Street, I was remaking my career. And I really thought that we were in very, very good shape. I really thought we were going to win this California thing. This went on for weeks and weeks, months and months. We got to D-Day, and we lost.

"I called him on the telephone, and I said, 'Ross, I hate to tell you this, but we've lost it.'

"And he said, 'Mort, the sun'll come up tomorrow. Come on back. Don't worry about it.'"

The bonds of that friendship are unbreakable. It was Perot who put up the first $10 million for the Dallas Symphony Hall. He gave the money with the stipulation that it be named the Morton H. Meyerson Symphony Hall.

"I worked on it for ten years," Meyerson says. "I am a great fan of classical music, and I go to all the great concert halls of Europe. I thought that there should be one in Dallas. It became a mission. We made the decision that we wanted great architecture, so we engaged I. M. Pei. We made the decision that we wanted great acoustics, we made the decision that we wanted to have a building that would be different. We wanted to build the first great symphony hall of the twentieth century.

"Well, I put in all this work, got it going, fought battles—battles about the size of the hall. If it gets too big, you can't have great acoustics. I argued the case to keep it small and intimate. Others argued economics. Every seat meant ten thousand dollars a year. At the last hour, both newspapers got into it, before it opened, calling it a rich person's deal. That was not going to help the citizens of Dallas. They pointed out that there were starving people in the streets. There were allegations that I was in bed with the city, conspiring to get around ordinances. There was an audit. They came back and said that instead of costing the projected $82 million, it cost $110 million. They were throwing in interest payments, parking garages—everything. It was a disaster.

"The criticism was relentless. They said we lost control of it, that there were fights between the architects, and in the last month, in August of 1989, the *Dallas Morning News* and the *Times Herald* came out with a three-part series, and the crux was that there was nothing good about the symphony hall.

"And I was talking to Ross the morning after the first one came out. At this point in time, I didn't work for him anymore. We'd see each other and talk on the phone a lot. But I saw him one morning, and he said, 'You look down. Are you mad about what's in the newspapers?'

"I said, 'Yeah, I really am. I'm so upset I wish my name wasn't on the building. I wish I'd never started this.'

"Ross turned to me, and he says, 'You know,

Mort, fifty years from now or a hundred years from now, when one of the best symphony halls is in Dallas, Texas, and they're writing reviews about how great it is, will it really make a difference whether this three-part article came out or not?' "

That stopped him. Meyerson smiled and put his arm around his old friend. "No, Ross, you're right, it really won't."

12

"It's not the critic who counts, not the man who points out how the strong man stumbled, or where the doer of deeds could have done them better. The credit belongs to the man who is actually in the arena; whose face is marred by dust and sweat and blood; who strives valiantly; who errs and comes up short again and again; who knows the great enthusiasms, the great devotions and who spends himself in a worthy cause; who at the best, knows in the end, the triumph of high achievement; and who, at the worst, if he fails, at least fails while daring greatly."

—ETCHED IN A BUST OF THEODORE ROOSEVELT OUTSIDE
PEROT'S OFFICE

The morning peace of the Perot log cabin on Lake Grapevine at Vail, Colorado, was broken by a telephone call on December 28, 1978, as Perot sat at breakfast with his family. Bill Gayden, president of the Perot subsidiary EDS World, was on the line from Dallas. The two top Perot men in Iran, Paul

Chiapparone and Bill Gaylord, had been arrested by the Iranian authorities.

"On what charges?" Perot asked.

"They didn't specify charges," said Gayden.

Perot's heart sank. His instinct had been to pull everyone out of Tehran three weeks before, when the shah's grip on the country seemed to have been finally broken. He had even gone into the Dallas office on December 4 after a sleepless night and declared, "Let's evacuate everyone." But his resolve had weakened and his staff, sensing it, had postponed action hoping that the shah would reestablish control. All too aware of his own failure to follow through, an icy, angry calm settled over Perot as he hammered out the questions: What law had his men been accused of breaking; who's doing what to get them out; how did this happen?

Then, as is his custom, he wanted everything done at once. He wanted Tom Luce in the office to begin work on the legalities of the men's seizure, he wanted contact with the State Department, he wanted a crisis team assembled to put some action plan together. He wanted lines opened to Washington and Tehran, and kept open. Someone should get in touch with Henry Kissinger, and with Kermit Roosevelt, who had been instrumental in the 1953

CIA coup that put the shah back on the throne. He wanted no stone unturned. He wanted assets in place, just in case; and no one dared to ask what he meant by that.

When finally he got off the phone that December morning, Perot announced he was going to take the four-wheel drive GM Suburban and catch a plane back to Dallas. "There's a blizzard out there," said Margot, who knew without his saying that he would go all the way to Iran. All she did say was "Drive carefully."

It was an unhappy time for Perot. His mother, Lulu May, lay dying back in Dallas. She was eighty-two, poignantly sick in Baylor Hospital where Ross junior had been born twenty years earlier. She had bone cancer and had broken a hip in a fall. On Christmas Day, unwilling to forgo the tradition, the family had loaded all the presents in a station wagon and held their annual party in the hospital. It was successful enough, with everyone putting the best face on things, but when the party was finished Lulu May had gotten testy. She had said she didn't want to see Ross the next day. Not that she was angry with him, but simply that she knew the family had plans to go to Vail and she did not want her illness to spoil everything. Ross had defied her, sent

Margot and the children off and stayed at his mother's bedside and waited for the rebuke he knew was coming.

You work hard, Lulu May had argued in that flat feisty voice that left no room for argument. Mother and son were in their eternal battle of wills. He might be the fabulous Ross Perot, mega-mogul-billionaire, to the rest of the world, but he was still her child, the son who backed off when she turned the glare of her authority in his direction. In 1968, for example, at the time when EDS went public, Ken Langone had suggested that, for business reasons, as well as appearances, Perot should remove Lulu May from the board of directors. Perot turned to his friend, grinned, and said, "You fire her."

Anyone who spent time around her knew that Lulu May was a force to be reckoned with. In December of 1969, when Ross was about to fly off to Hanoi to help the prisoners of war, he came to her to talk about something nagging him. If he went, he said, the price of EDS stock might plunge because of his escapade. Could he, in all conscience, do that to the shareholders? Wasn't he morally obliged to take their welfare into account, as well as the convictions he held so tightly? As Ken Follett wrote in his bestselling book *On Wings of Eagles*, her reply came without hesitation: "Let them sell their shares."

In Dallas she had won the confrontation with her stubborn son. She had an emotional advantage lying there with the tubes running in and out of her and her tiny five-foot frame lost in the white sheets of the tall hospital bed. The next day Ross had succumbed to her steely resolve, as he usually did, and joined the rest of the family in Vail—as it happened, for only a few hours of recreation before the phone call that plunged him into the riskiest adventure of his life.

Perot's involvement with Iran began in the summer of 1976, when the shah had asked EDS to install a modern health-care and social-security system for Iran's 33 million citizens. A few hundred engineers and their families had been sent from Dallas. Computerizing the payroll deductions and benefit systems was easy enough in itself, given their skills, but the beginning had been almost as tough as the ending. They had to devise a program to issue a social-security card to everyone in a country without records, files, or basic information systems. Without an administrative infrastructure, the work had proved slow and exasperating and the costs had run

to about $1.4 million a month, which was fine when
the shah was running the country, but worrisome
when the ministers who were supposedly responsible were arrested or vanished. The bills of $1.4 mil-
lion a month began to pile up unpaid, and Perot
refused to indulge the usual practice of paying
back-alley bribes to get things done. The middlemen and shakedown artists did not quite grasp the
high principles at issue; they wrote it off as stingi-
ness. In any event, by November, two months after
the declaration of martial law, Iran owed EDS
World $4 million.

Perot's people had been warning him about the
growing instability of the shah's rule, long before
the State Department woke to the change. They
were closer to the people than the diplomats inside
their "secure" compound. Perot was impressed with
the way a certain blindness afflicted the people who
worked in foreign embassies, so that instead of representing the United States, they become surrogate
representatives of the host country. "The State Department people never left the embassy," says Perot
sharply. "They had no idea what was going on."
The EDS people met the Iranians in the markets
and in their homes. They knew that leases were not
being renewed for homes rented to Westerners, that

no one wanted to cook or clean or work in any way for the Americans. People who had been friends one day were cold the next. The Muslim fundamentalists were acting bolder, as if their leader, the ayatollah Khomeini, had already returned from his Paris exile. It was so different from the honeymoon days, when the EDS people came in as saviors, and were treated like royalty. Or at least guests of royalty.

Soon EDS World had foreseen enough of the impending emergency to evacuate most of its 130 families, but some key company men, like Chiapparone and Gaylord, had remained behind to safeguard equipment and company interests. They bore the heat of pressing their legitimate claims, confronted by more radical officials who began to make vague accusations that EDS's pretax profits of 20 percent were exorbitant. As Christmas approached, the streets were inflamed with riots, shootings, and firebombings, then Chiapparone and Gaylord were ordered to report to a government office on December 28. They were interrogated all day and thrown into a cell. Bail was set at $12,750,000—the approximate amount still owed on the unfinished contract.

Four days after their arrest, and the breakfast call to Vail, Colonel Arthur D. ("Bull") Simons, retired, was roused at 2 A.M. by a call from Dallas. Would he be willing to go to Tehran to rescue two people? Ken Follett reports his answer: "When we do we start?"

Perot and Simons were more alike than not—in spite of the fact that Bull was six feet tall and had the torso of a blockhouse and the hands of a steam shovel. Like Perot, he was a passionate believer in direct action. Like Perot, he advertised it in his style. He wore his hair in a brisk military crew cut, which, on a man of his years (sixty then) and unforgiving countenance, carried a look of menace. The two men of derring-do had met almost a decade earlier after Arthur D. Simons, then an army colonel, had led a commando raid on the Son Tay prisoner-of-war camp twenty-three miles outside of Hanoi. There were no prisoners at the camp and the raid was dismissed by many as ludicrous, but Ross Perot, better than anyone, appreciated the gallantry that went into the execution. It wasn't Bull Simons's fault that the intelligence was flawed and the camp empty.

The other factor that aroused Perot's underdog, defiant sympathies was that Simons had trouble advancing in an army still vaguely anti-Semitic (Simons was Jewish) and squeamish about promoting wild daredevils to the rank of general. But of some things there was no doubt: The soldiers who served under Simons would follow him into hell; he always brought back his men; and his planning for any mission was meticulous. Perot recognized these prized qualities after the Bull had retired from the service, when Ross sponsored another Simons mission into Laos to try to find POWs in 1974.

After the Vietnam War ended, and Perot sponsored a parade and weekend party in San Francisco for the returning prisoners of war, he invited Bull Simons and his Son Tay Raiders. One of the celebrity guests was John Wayne, who shook the colonel's hand and said in awe, "You are the man I play in the movies."

But that had been years ago, and now Simons, who had a bad heart and had suffered a small stroke even before the Son Tay Raid, was raising pigs on a farm in the Florida Panhandle. He felt he had lost his reason for living when his wife, Lucille, died ten months earlier. His hair had grown long, he ate cold food out of cans, and when he looked at the farm, he thought of burning it down.

The two A.M. call on the second day of 1979 had come from T. J. Marquez, a vice president of EDS in Dallas. It marked a defeat for Perot's counsel,

Tom Luce, who had been running around the EDS headquarters trying to convince his boss that this notion of a private rescue attempt would head him into a hurricane of legal trouble. Luce had pointed out all the pitfalls: the fact that what Perot was talking about was a mercenary force in which everyone could be shot if they were caught; the fact that they would be abandoning the legal protections of citizenship by waging what amounted to war on a sovereign nation; the fact that they would be giving up their single most potent weapon—namely that the prisoners were completely innocent and had not done anything wrong; the fact that if Perot went ahead he would be disowned by his government, denounced by the press, destroyed in the marketplace, or imprisoned by one side or the other. Take your pick.

Perot's response had been typically cryptic: "I've thought of all that."

Luce, in retrospect, says he admired exactly the way Perot went about it all.

"Number one, he made sure that someone was charged with exhausting every legal and political route to get the men free. But simultaneously, he called Colonel Simons; he put in place a parallel track, but he was very prudent about it. He always knew it was risky. He said, 'People's lives will be risked if I ever utilize that option. So it's my last option.'"

And then he uttered his last argument, one from which he would not retreat: "But, Tom, I'm not going to abandon those men."

Tom Luce was a demon on the international calls, the legal agenda, the political muscle. He even tried to pay the $12,750,000 ransom, but no bank was willing to move a letter of credit quickly. And one day, as he and Perot were together, Ross's secretary, Sally Bell, poked her head in the office and said, "It's Henry Kissinger on the phone."

Perot heard the sound of a familiar frog croaking in his ear. "I have been assured that your men will be released tomorrow at ten A.M.," Kissinger said.

"That's just the best news I've heard since I don't know when," gushed Perot, puffed up with gratitude.

A high State Department official called to confirm the news later, but when ten o'clock Tehran time came and went and the man stationed outside the Ministry of Justice saw no one emerge, everyone in the EDS camp in Dallas deflated.

"I'm convinced Kissinger talked to the shah," says Tom Luce now. "I'm convinced that the shah said, 'I'll release them.' But that just proved to us that the shah wasn't really in power. Because when the order went down, nothing happened. That's when we were all convinced that there was not a structure or government for us to deal with."

Ross Perot nodded, listened, and knew that this was the time to start putting into operation the riskier track. He had no other choice. This was the hour to turn loose Bull Simons.

13

"When you need a job done, you get together a small team and go with them all the way."

—ROSS PEROT

It was an eight-man team of Vietnam veterans, all volunteers and ten years away from combat. They were soldiers in the corporate wars now, not hunter-killers stalking an enemy through steamy jungles in Southeast Asia.

Almost all had had military training, all were accustomed to discipline, and beyond that, all were committed to following Ross Perot, if not Bull Simons. But the years of soft living had taken a toll, and when they went out to Ross's house on Lake Grapevine to try to work some of the kinks out of their creaky bones, it was a lot more effort than they thought.

As if that weren't enough, they were reminded by

the sight of the Walther PPK pistols that they were all married men with children, accustomed to business suits and white shirts rather than khaki camouflage, and about to engage in a desperate act.

Simons went over the personnel folders.

Joe Poché would be the driver. He was thirty-two and had spent six years in the army and commanded an artillery unit in Vietnam. He knew weapons and tactics and had spent two years in Iran. He was a tight-lipped guy who was smart and patient, but lacked a sense of humor. Ralph Boulware would ride shotgun. He had nine years in the air force and knew about inboard computers, but no one knew how much, if anything, he knew about combat.

Jim Schwebach, at age thirty-five, was ex-Special Forces. A commando. He had spent eleven years in the service and knew about explosives and weapons. And he was a fighter, reliable in a pinch. He would be a flank guard in any operation.

Pat Sculley looked good on paper. He had been a captain in the Rangers, but he had no combat experience.

Glenn Jackson had no military experience, but he was a hunter and he knew Tehran and he was enthusiastic. Jay Coburn was a former helicopter pilot

wounded in Vietnam who would be second in command to Bull Simons. He was forever in debt to
Ross Perot for saving his infant son when he needed
a heart operation. Ron Davis at thirty was the youngest in the group. He would ride point at whatever
object Simons aimed at. He had some knowledge of
Farsi, and while he had no military training, he was
a black belt in karate. Each had to contend with the
real possibility that he would soon be engaged in
violent confrontations or legal wrangles or any of a
dozen nameless complications.

As Margot said, life with Ross would never be
dull.

At the house on Grapevine Lake, Simons showed
the men how to kill quickly and silently using a
Gerber knife. He demonstrated a lethal technique
by pointing out a spot on Glenn Jackson's back
where the kidneys were located. "Won't they cry
out?" someone asked. "No," replied Simons,
"they'll be in too much pain." He spoke softly but
firmly about the dangers and the fears that lay
ahead. You had to be afraid in such an operation. If
you weren't, you were lying or psycho. He didn't
want anyone with either attribute along. They had
enough with which to contend. But it was okay.
They were all properly terrified.

The intelligence and plans of the city and news of the hostages arrived daily from the telephone link to Tehran. Codes were devised, messages passed, visits made to Gasr Prison, where the men were being held. EDS still had a few friends, as well as some ground staff in Iran.

And along the way, Simons developed a plan. There would be a diversionary attack and then a direct assault on the jail, which appeared poorly and halfheartedly defended. The escape from the country would be made through a United States Air Force base, where they would be safe. False documents were prepared. Cover stories were invented. Timetables were arranged so that the last legal and diplomatic effort could be given a fair chance.

During the early stages of the planning, Ross junior, then twenty, passed through the EDS office in Dallas and saw the unmistakable frantic preparations. His father took him aside and made Ross junior promise that he would leave school and raise his sisters in the event of an "accident."

"I saw the look in my father's eyes," recalls Ross junior, "and I knew enough to just say, 'Yes, sir.'"

There was one other stop Ross Perot had to make. He went to see his mother. As Ken Follett describes the scene, it was Ross who had to fight back emotion. "She knew she was dying," Follett wrote. "And she knew that, even if Perot should come back alive and well after a few days, she might no longer be there. Cancer was rapidly destroying her body, but there was nothing wrong with her mind, and her sense of right and wrong was as clear as ever. 'You don't have a choice, Ross,' she had said. 'They're your men. You sent them over there. They didn't do anything wrong. Our government won't help them. *You* are responsible for them. It's up to you to get them out. You have to go.'"

Whatever else they were talking about, they were saying good-bye. Bette recalls it as one of the rare times she saw tears in her brother's eyes.

Perot made his way to Paris and then Jordan. Posing as a television news courier for NBC, he flew into Iran. He passed through customs easily and remembered something that Jan, a dazzlingly handsome ski instructor, told him once at Vail when the women all turned in Jan's direction. It was the burden of striking good looks. "You're lucky, Ross," the Norwegian instructor said. "When you walk into a room, no one notices you."

At the time, Perot wasn't grateful for the compliment, but as he eased his way through the tense

Tehran airport without attracting attention, he changed his mind. He passed through the road-blocks on his way to the hotel in downtown Tehran, driving by burning cars and armed militia, and adopted an air of tranquil detachment. The ground team left behind to look after EDS affairs had taken rooms at the Hyatt Crown Regency. In his spare time, Perot mapped an emergency escape route. There were some staff members from EDS World who were handling the logistics, but no one dared ask Perot, "What, exactly, are you doing here?"

It made no sense. He was the multimillionaire head of an American corporation—the very symbol of everything that the fundamentalist militants and mullahs had been preaching against. A great big capitalist villain! He would make, as Luce had noted, an excellent hostage.

But it was important for Ross Perot to be there in Tehran, at the knifepoint of danger. To see it with his own eyes. To feel it. To share with the men he had sent there the hazards of the game. He couldn't explain it—not completely—it sounded too juvenile. But he knew that he was right to come. His intuition told him that.

He knocked on the door of Keane Taylor, one of

the team handling logistics, and said, "Bring me up to speed."

There were plans and efforts and contacts. It was all very evasive, with men appearing in the morning who claimed that they had influence in whatever new government was running things. But by afternoon they evaporated like morning mist. The truth was that events were reeling out of control. No one could make anything happen. Not by issuing an order. Not by regular channels.

By January 19, Ross Perot had figured out something that he could do. He could visit the men in jail. As Follett writes, "It was a little crazy," but it was crazy brave, and there was nothing else that would demonstrate his dedication, or his resourcefulness, to the men behind bars. But Perot knew something that the EDS men on the ground didn't: that the chaos worked in his favor. He could walk into the prison because no one knew who he was, and even if some people did, it would be the last thing they would expect. There was one other factor, something he told Tom Luce and that anyone who studied his life would guess: He was lucky.

But when he got to the prison, he thought that his luck had run out. For there at the gate to the prison was an American television camera crew. He tucked his head down, concentrating on the small cardboard box he was carrying. It was loaded with warm clothes, books, and some food. He signed the guest book, "H. R. Perot," showed his passport, and ran smack into someone he knew. It was Ramsey Clark, the former attorney general under Lyndon Johnson, and a Texan who had met Ross Perot many times over the years. Without breaking stride, Perot walked over to Clark, stuck out his hand, and said, "Hello, Ramsey, what are you doing in jail?"

The six-foot-three Clark looked down and laughed and shook Perot's hand. "How's Mimi?" Perot asked, referring to Clark's sister, who was a close friend of Ross and Margot.

"Mimi's fine," replied Clark.

"Well, good to see you," said Perot, and marched off into the prison. He noticed that the Iranian general to whom Clark had been talking was whispering in Farsi to an aide. With Perot were Jay Coburn and Rich Gallagher, an administrative assistant—one of the volunteers who stayed behind with his wife, Cathy, to help extract his boss, Paul Chiapparone.

They were not unmasked. Slightly befuddled, Ramsey Clark, it turned out, thought that he had run into Eastern Airlines president Frank Borman at the Gasr Prison. Inside, the two hostages were grateful to see Perot, but hesitant about the break-out. Perot laid down the law, which was the only law that seemed to be working in Iran at the time. Escaping seemed to be the only way for them to get loose. Otherwise, they could be put on trial, exe-cuted . . . there was no telling.

Meanwhile, the team under Bull Simons was set-tled into the hotel, not moving out for fear of dis-covery. But one day Simons and one of the Iranian engineer trainees walked over to the prison, while the colonel gave his young friend a lecture about the French Revolution and how the peasants rose up and stormed the Bastille, which was the symbol of oppression.

He planted the idea that when such a thing hap-pened in Tehran—which the trainee "Rashid" as-sured him it would—someone reliable ought to be on hand to guide Paul and Bill back to safety. Rashid took the hint and assigned himself that role. Simons had taken note that the jail was more heav-ily defended than he'd expected, and he was unwill-ing to risk the lives of his men on a foolish gesture. Meanwhile, until the negotiating situation clarified itself, the "rescue" team waited impatiently in hotel rooms.

*   *   *

The ayatollah Khomeini returned to Iran at the start of February, and on Friday, February 9, the country came apart. Khomeini had called for the military to mutiny, Parliament to resign, and the public to support him. He had appointed a provisional government, and one by one, military units began to switch loyalty to the fundamentalists.

The next day, as a letter of credit for $12,750,000 was ready to be issued through the Bank of Oman, a strange mood hit the city. Word of a general strike for Monday was passed like an electric current. Bull Simons said to one of the team, "Tomorrow's the day!" He had already scouted an escape route by land through Turkey.

On the day of the strike, Rashid left his home and passed the armory, then, on impulse, went in and began handing out rifles to the citizens. It was like the French Revolution. A rumor swept by that Evin Prison had been liberated and that now it was the turn of the Gasr Prison. Marching to Gasr Square, Rashid shouted to his ragtag army, "The Gasr Prison is our Bastille!" A roar went up from the crowd, and shooting began in the square.

Prison guards resisted halfheartedly, then fled. The prison was open! Rashid squeezed through a window and began searching for Paul and Bill among the 11,800 inmates.

He didn't find them for the simple reason that they had made their own way out and through the mad streets to the Hyatt.

Ross was waiting in Ankara, Turkey, as the rescue team—dubbed the "Dirty Team"—piled into a small caravan and drove with Paul and Bill through bandit country, full of insurgents, loyalists, and confused refugees. Rashid had faked an official letter of transit, and the team drove north through Kurdish strongholds.

Meanwhile, the ground personnel who had been staying in Iran legally, the so-called "Clean Team," cleared up the hotel bill and raced for the airport. They were trying to be out of the country before the Iranian "negotiators," who seemed always to be trying to extract the maximum amount of money and inflict the optimum amount of frustration on their American victims, realized that all of EDS had vanished from their midst.

As the hapless diplomats at the American embassy endured waves of confusion and changing ranks of authority, Perot moved a bus to the Turkish-Iranian border and waited for the Dirty Team to emerge from the chaos. Simons was bulling his way through checkpoints, talking his way out of scrapes, flattering Kurdish opponents of the regime, as the convoy made its way northwest through the Elburz Mountains. At one point, they were arrested and put on trial before a "revolutionary committee." Rashid bluffed his way through the crisis by saying he was a delegate from the Tehran Revolutionary Committee and that a decision had been made to expel all Americans. He was simply enforcing the will of the ayatollah.

Telephone lines to Tehran were down, and so the Dirty Team was not discovered and inched north, to safety.

At the border town of Rezaiyeh, teenage guards with rifles stood between them and Turkey. At fifteen minutes before midnight of February 15, 1970, Colonel Simons, fed up with every local chief's chest-pounding bullying, took his team and simply stepped over a chain fence and walked into Turkey. "Don't look back and don't stop for anything," he instructed everyone. It was that simple.

On the other side was a bus to carry them to freedom.

Lulu May Perot died on April 3, 1979. A little more than a month later, Colonel Bull Simons's heart gave out, and he died on May 21, after spending the final weeks of his life at the guest cottage on Perot's Dallas estate. On November 4, 1979, despite the best efforts of the Jimmy Carter administration to placate the Iranian fundamentalists, militants over-ran the embassy, and fifty-two hostages were held for 444 days. Ross Perot thought that he might have gotten them out, and he was consulted, but then he changed his mind when he ran up against sputtering bean counters who were in charge of the official rescue operation.

"Sometimes," he said afterward, "you gotta trust what you feel."

14

"An activist is the guy who cleans the river, not the guy who concludes it's dirty."

—ONE OF ROSS PEROT'S FAVORITE EPIGRAMS

He was always conspicuous by a certain bold strut (not that he ever lacked self-confidence), but after Tehran, Ross Perot became downright cocky. He began to believe that fortune would always blush favorably on his undertakings.

"I'm not a living legend," he said when NBC's Maria Shriver called him one. "I'm just a myth."

Myths require tending, and Perot had decided that he had other patches of the garden to cultivate. More and more, he turned over the everyday duties of running EDS to Morton Meyerson, who became president of the company in 1979. Perot, though still the biggest stockholder of the company, was free to bloom elsewhere.

＊   ＊   ＊

The rueful consequences of Perot's wandering attention were quick in coming. Within a matter of weeks, his celebrated, high-tech computer commandos fell smack on their keyboards in Illinois through a number of asinine miscalculations. Not that they hadn't followed a plan, gone through a careful system of checks and evaluations. They had been faithful to all the rules. It was just the old bugaboo that no one can remove from calculations—the human factor. In Illinois, EDS proved that they were human.

EDS had made a low bid of $41.8 million for a five-year contract to process claims in the Illinois Medicare program. In April 1979, fresh from the victory in Iran, the EDS engineers and programmers and management wizards moved into their chosen headquarters at Des Plaines, outside of Chicago. They promptly realized that they had made a big mistake. A spokesman at the time called it "one of the worst management decisions" they ever made. The suburban town of Des Plaines had been selected because EDS planners thought that there would be a big labor pool waiting to snatch the four hundred jobs they had to fill. However, they hadn't studied unemployment in Des Plaines—they used unemployment statistics for the greater Chicago region. Everyone in Des Plaines already had a job.

Okay, no problem—just pull in some hackers from the nearby suburbs. Big problem. That was one of the tricks of the suburban mass transit system in that part of Chicago: You couldn't get there from here. Although they conducted three separate site studies, the planners did not pick up on this crucial detail. "If you know about Chicago, you know you can go from any suburb into the city and back out very efficiently," an EDS spokesman explained ruefully. "But if you want to go from one suburb to another suburb—forget it."

The company looked ridiculous.

But the real price was paid by the senior citizens of Illinois. In six months there was a backlog of 454,000 claims for Illinois Medicare payments and the rate of error in the claims was an embarrassing 25 percent—one in four. Contractual penalties piled up to $700,000.

That April 1979 proved the starting point of another rescue mission, with results more dubious than those of the Iranian episode. It began in the East Texas town of Tyler, not far from Texarkana, which was having a drug problem. The local officials hired Craig Matthews—an experienced detective—to act as an undercover narc. Matthews brought in a policewoman, Kim Ramsey (later to become his wife), to complete his cover assignments.

The Tyler "problem" began after a raid on April 25, when more than one hundred alleged dealers and drug users were rounded up, essentially on evidence supplied by Matthews and Ramsey. Later, in September, after a summer of testimony, there was a horrifying incident in which someone attacked the couple in their isolated trailer with a shotgun. The blast critically wounded Matthews.

The two cops asserted that they were the target of a professional assassin. Perot, quick to support military, paramilitary, or embattled law-enforcement officials, raced onto the scene. He surrounded the couple with armed guards in dark suits (men who even accompanied them into the judge's chambers when they had a conference), and provided them with a safe house.

"They badly needed protection," proclaimed Perot. "I gave it to them."

When it was revealed later that Matthews and Ramsey had themselves been drug abusers and had doctored evidence, they were jailed and Perot was humiliated. Nevertheless, Perot felt he had done the right thing—even if it turned out to be embarrassing. If cops were in peril, he'd be there. "I have told the chief of police in Dallas that any policeman gets hurt, send me the bill," he said recently.

The public failure of the Tyler episode did not spoil Perot's invincible, boyish disposition. Nothing did. For instance, when he wanted to tweak Army at an Army-Navy football game during the early seventies, he and some of his Praetorian Guard slipped into the barracks at West Point and plastered BEAT ARMY posters on the walls. He even managed to corrupt the Army chaplain and got into the bell tower, where he rigged the bells to ring "Anchors Aweigh" and "The Marine Corps Hymn." When he was arrested by an MP, he was released from the West Point stockade on the condition that he not return.

Such antics kept him amused. He was having "fun," as he said was the duty and obligation of all human beings. He thrived on pranks and hijinks. When Ken Follett was contracted to write *On Wings of Eagles* about the Iran rescue operation, Perot found out which plane he'd be on when he was coming to Texas. He reserved two seats on either side of Follett. Then he had two of the best-looking women in the office take the seats flanking Follett, and, acting as if they were strangers to each other, the women each gushed shamelessly over the author's looks, talents, and sweet nature. The British author of *The Key to Rebecca* was so taken in that when Ross junior later asked which city, after London, was his favorite, Follett replied without hesitation: Dallas.

At Follett's wedding, Perot sent another woman to Follett's home with a pillow under her dress. She introduced herself to his bride as Follett's wife and began crying. It was all very playful and harmless locker-room behavior, but sometimes it actually did some good. When the navy asked Perot if he could arrange a show for the Mediterranean fleet and get, say, Wayne Newton to appear, Perot was aghast.

"Unless things have changed a lot in the navy since my days, I have a better idea," wrote Perot, who then flew all the contestants in the Miss U.S.A. contest to the ship.

But in July 1980, Perot got another harsh and unexpected lesson. Ross and the family were in London on vacation when he got a call that jolted him back to reality: EDS, he was told, had lost the Texas Medicaid contract, the linchpin of the company's business empire.

The contract would have enabled the computer

company to handle the $2 billion of state and federal money to be spent on medical care for the poor between 1981 and 1985. Although they were faced with losses amounting to roughly $15 million annually, the blow to the company's prestige would be incalculable. There was no telling what could follow. Already people in the industry were saying that EDS was no longer an invincible, efficient number-crunching giant. This would evoke . . . pity.

Perot immediately got on a plane back to Dallas. He was not going to let this happen without a fight. It was like the old days, when he was just starting out at IBM or creating EDS out of thin air. The first thing he did was assign legal responsibility for handling the fiasco to John L. Hill, who had powerful political connections. Then he visited Governor Bill Clements, Texas attorney general Mark White, and all the members of the state's Human Resources Board, as well as two members of the Human Resources Department. He was within the law, but he was calling in all the markers. It may not have been entirely proper, but it was pushing the envelope.

Then he started putting real pressure on members of the Texas Human Resources Board, which decides on the contracts. Three times in the next few days, Perot and Meyerson flew by helicopter to the cattle ranch and rice farm of lame-duck Democrat Hilmar Moore, who was board chairman. It was a sight to see, that chopper dropping down out of the sky, and it always left an impression. The rancher had to think that he was important to rate such a visit, and he had to be a little intimidated, like maybe he was about to be hit by airborne computer commandos.

Day and night, Perot and Meyerson visited each key player in the contract battle, blasting them with studies and statistics, challenging the basis for the award.

Their pitch was always the same. The Human Resources Board staff's interpretation that the Bradford National Corporation's bid was lowest was based on faulty data. "We used the documents that [they] had already seen," Perot recalled afterward in an interview in *Barron's*, "and explained where these documents were wrong . . . that the [Human Resources] staff had misrepresented the figures by adding forecasts that had no significance and turned EDS from the low bidder to the high bidder."

Hilmar Moore was out of his depth. "All I have ever been told was that it was a complicated mathematical formula," he told *Barron's*. "It is too deep for me."

It might have been over his head, but Perot's word was good enough for him to change his vote. "Ross never told me a thing that's not true," Moore said recently.

The fight continued at a terrific pitch, with Bradford and EDS hurling conflicting numbers, claims, and accusations at each other. Ultimately, a bid-evaluation committee found both companies equally qualified, giving a slight edge to Bradford. But EDS was family. And that gave Perot the decisive advantage. It should have been plain on the evening of July 29, when Peter Del Col, the head of Bradford, walked into an Austin chamber to pitch his contract; he knew before a word was uttered that he was out of his element.

"I started my presentation, and out of twenty or thirty people in the room, I was the only one wearing a jacket and tie," Del Col said. "I was looking at T-shirts and polo shirts."

Clearly he didn't know the territory. Months earlier, unbeknownst to Del Col, Texas governor Bill Clements had banned suit jackets and neckties in state buildings during the summer in order to save money on air conditioning.

In the end, the board went with a known quantity, EDS. "The question the board had is how you can evaluate an unknown against the reality of what you know," argued Gerald Chapman, the Human Resources commissioner. "I imagine the chairman would weigh heavily in favor of someone he had worked with before in the care of his cattle rather than someone who had a paper plan."

Hilmar Moore tried to find some consoling aspect to the free-for-all. As he told *Barron's:* "Out of all this it is reassuring to me that—in spite of all the poor government we have got, primarily in Washington but it spills over other places—in spite of all that, the free-enterprise system is still working. And if you throw two billion dollars up there for grabs, there damn sure are some dogs that will bite for it."

The battle with Bradford had woken the slumbering street fighter in Ross Perot. But soon his attention drifted again. Though he might deny it to close friends, he was a fireman without a fire, a conqueror with no more worlds to conquer. He lashed out over puny issues unworthy of his wrath. He wanted to build a helipad on his estate, claiming that he had had death threats during the Tyler drug controversy, but neighbors—principally J. F. Bucy, head of Texas

Instruments—fought it off on the grounds that it would be noisy and unnecessary, and might even turn the neighborhood into a shooting gallery. The city Planning Commission stood up to Perot and denied him permission.

Then, in 1982, Perot paid for the design of the Vietnam War memorial wall in Washington, D.C. He sparked controversy when he insisted that a representational statue be built to accompany it. "I thought there should be something for the survivors," he says.

Not long after, he sponsored his son on a round-the-world helicopter flight, leasing a freighter to refuel Ross junior's single-engine Bell Ranger helicopter, which had its 350-mile range extended to 800 miles when the Soviets refused landing rights in the Pacific.

Then, in 1984, hearing of the financial plight of the family holding an original copy of the Magna Carta, Perot dispatched Tom Luce to England to bring it back. The 687-year-old document was in the hands of relatives of the Earl of Cardigan—the man who led the Charge of the Light Brigade. It was one of seventeen copies known to exist, but the most complete version of the updated Magna Carta issued by King Edward I on October 12, 1297. (The

first Magna Carta was issued by King John at Run-
nymede, granting rights of man before law under
threat of civil war.)

The Brudenell family, strapped for funds, had
been trying to sell the parchment since it was discovered in 1974 during an inventory of family
records at the ten-thousand-acre Northamptonshire
manor, Deene Park. When Marian Brudenell first
told British Museum authorities that she had an
authentic version of the document, they reacted
with scorn. "They were so patronizing," Marian told
a reporter. "They treated me pityingly, as a half-
witted girl." They were under the impression that it
was a Victorian reproduction.

When museum experts finally authenticated the
document, they offered a mere $23,000; the
Brudenell family turned it down.

Perot paid $1.5 million for the document and do-
nated it to the National Archives.

"I thought it was interesting we could have that
in our country. Of course it's not about the rights
of the average man; it was written in Latin and the
average man couldn't read Latin."

15

"The Japanese have a great saying: 'When the student is ready, the Buddha will appear.'"

—MORT MEYERSON

It is Mort Meyerson's unswerving belief that Ross Perot is not a strict technocrat who simply manages a big company, keeping his eye on the moving parts and simultaneously focusing on the bottom-line profits. "No one can do that," he says. "Not with fifty thousand employees and a hundred projects."

Complex computer technology is a more intricate, elegant thing than a mere mechanical trick, according to Meyerson. Someone who runs a really large enterprise has to sense the patterns and movements of business and culture in the same way that a great whale will navigate by feeling the shifting currents in the ocean. It is, in short, not completely rational, but a sensuous, intuitive thing. You can

design systems and set some operations in motion
but ultimately no one can control so many employees and so many programs.

What Perot does, and what he does better than
anyone else, Meyerson believes, is set the wheels in
motion, get the thing spinning, then trust that the
perceived patterns will hold. It is a kind of techno-
mystical art that cannot be taught or learned, or, in
most cases, even grasped. It seems chaotic and sug-
gestive of a random universe, but it's not. If it
works, it adheres to certain internal laws that can be
understood only in the most subtle way. That is
only someone who has uncanny sensory gifts can
operate such a company.

"When you've got a four-billion-dollar business
and when you've got thousands of customers and
millions of transactions a second moving all over
the place, and when you've got every regulatory
agency in the universe on your case, and when
you've got to do business in foreign countries which
have different cultural values; when you have
changes in the shareholding world about what their
attitudes are toward companies, that's not a rational
world," says Meyerson.

"That is an irrational world. It's the same world
as if you were governor of Texas or if you were presi-

dent of the United States. The difference is a matter of scale."

Ross Perot was unhappy with his scale. After he had put EDS back in orbit by winning back the Medicaid contract, he was, perhaps, bored, needing new challenges. All his companies were pirouetting nicely, bringing in lots of profits, but the operation no longer required high-wire acts of administrative daring on his part. The business almost ran itself.

Consider his anti-drug stance. Perot was in Turkey, waiting for his rescue team to come out of Iran, when Governor Bill Clements appointed him to head a citizens' committee to wage a war on illegal substances. He heard about the appointment from one of his employees. "I knew you'd accept," Clements told him. He flung himself into battle. He raided his own company for volunteers and sent them to the four corners of the state to study the problem. And when they all returned and presented their reports, Perot thought about it, then came to his own conclusions.

"You know, you can talk all day, but the plain fact was this thing was ruining a lot of lives and you had to take some drastic action," he says. "You could have a lot of people complaining, or you could do something. I proposed to do something."

He was influenced by Margot's volunteer work. She'd seen a lot of pain and suffering in the inner cities among children from dysfunctional families.

It was painful, but Margot learned about the plagues of drugs and abuse and incest and she spoke of these things to her husband in her oblique, refined and overpoweringly convincing manner.

Because he was a direct and impatient man, Perot wanted to deal with these infinitely complex problems in his own blunt fashion. The first thing he did was draft EDS attorney Richard Salwen to rewrite the Texas criminal code. Perot had decided that the current laws didn't do the job. They were entirely too lenient when it came to the first step—marijuana. If you were permissive about that, then users would inevitably slip onto the next step . . . and the next. So he wanted very tough penalties for marijuana pushers. After that, he assisted Nancy Reagan in her "Just say no!" campaign. There were, in all, five bills prepared by Salwen. Intentionally Draconian, with long mandatory sentencing for dealers to discourage drug distribution to youth, they were quickly passed by the Austin legislature.

Perot's antidrug positions have prompted controversy. Though he denies ever saying it, there are those who attest that Perot once told a Dallas meeting that there would be no way to solve the problem unless you cordoned off certain sections of town—areas notorious for drug use—and went house to house rooting out violators. It would not be pretty and would not be popular, but then neither was the problem.

Another Perot target was a partnership close to sacred on Texas soil: education and the school sports programs. In 1984, the Texas education establishment was ruled by what was called the "iron triangle." It consisted of the House and Senate legislative committees, education bureaucracies (the Texas Education Agency), and unions representing teachers and coaches. The new governor, Mark White, asked Perot to serve as chairman of the Select Committee on Public Education (SCOPE). The governor had no idea that the so-called camel's nose he had let under the tent would raise such a storm.

Using his own money, Perot brought in experts on education. "World-class people," he says. "I wanted to know where we were headed."

Perot's specialists found that teachers were poorly paid and needed a lot more special compensation.

They found that extracurricular activities were important. But this husband and brother of former teachers was listening for something else.

"The only folks I met that really talked about educating children were teachers and those wonderful elementary-school principals," he says now.

What astonished him was the complacency of the high school principals, who thought that the existing after-school programs (football, mostly) were perfect. Perot went to town, attacking the football establishment. He denounced the presence of football coaches at the top level of academic management. "It was the football comments that got the most ink," he told *Texas Business*, "but we were also taking a hard look at such cost-ineffective programs as vocational and agricultural education."

He drove home his points to reporters and writers with down-home wisdom and dry wit:

"I have a documented case of one boy [traveling] sixty-five days across Texas with a chicken [to attend a livestock show]. . . . The chicken was worn out. A chicken can only take so much travel.

"Extracurricular activities are about the only place in the public school system where we demand excellence from our children. . . .

"I thought I was living pretty well until I found

out that high school football players have towel warmers."

The howl of pain from the alumni, the fans, the coaches, and the ex-coaches rang from one end of the state to the other. Perot, meanwhile, in his picolo-piper voice, lobbied for a bill that would prevent students from participating in after-school sports unless they had passing grades. He rallied the business community and the politicians for a school reform package. And he won.

This victory came in the midst of behind-the-scenes negotiations to sell EDS. In April 1984, John Gutfreund, the CEO of Salomon Brothers, called and asked Perot if he was interested in a merger with General Motors.

"When a company the size of GM approaches," Perot told one reporter, "you have to consider it.

"I thought I misunderstood him at first. If he had said AT&T was interested, I'd have understood. But GM?"

Meyerson handled the day-to-day negotiations with General Motors while Perot finished up his education report. And when he finally met Roger Smith, chairman of General Motors, there was a spark of recognition. They were both tough, ornery types who took no prisoners and brooked no defeat. They both had spit in their eye, but each thought he could tame the other.

When the deal went through in October (Perot received an estimated $2.5 billion for his 50 percent interest), Smith thought that he was acquiring EDS and Perot thought that a true merger had taken place. His EDS firm would provide computer models for designing high-tech cars, for administrative reforms, for modernizing the assembly lines with efficient techniques. "We want to produce the best car in the world," he said. "That's what business should do."

He was given a seat on the board of directors, and it was not a token sinecure. He spent his weekends in his khaki slacks and baseball cap, touring GM dealerships, where, unrecognized, he saw the way customers were treated. And he toured production plants and spoke to the workers on the line.

"He's livened up the board meetings quite a bit," a laughing Charles Townes, a physics professor and fellow board member, told *The New York Times*.

Roger Smith was not amused. Perot kept saying publicly that the management of GM had no interest in what kind of car they produced. "I could never understand why it takes six years to build a car when it only took us four years to win World War II," he quipped.

Smith boiled, pointed out that GM had forty times the earnings that EDS pulled in. But Perot was forever sounding off, complaining about the slow methods and tedious routine of the GM operation. He even refused to take a free car—a perk provided every three months to board members. He heard that the directors' cars were getting special inspections and he wanted to see what they were like off the lot.

"That's what I am—an irritant around here," he told the *Times*. "I stir things up."

In December 1986, using all the leverage he could muster, Roger Smith forced Perot off GM's board of directors. So great was the irritant that Smith bought Perot's remaining shares for $750 million in return for his leaving. Perot departed, but not without tweaking Roger Smith once more by saying that he would put the money in an escrow account in case they changed their minds.

They didn't. In 1988, Perot launched a flock of new companies under the umbrella of the Perot Group, all making money or accumulating real estate. The linchpin was his donation of land for a commercial airport in Fort Worth, which would be built by federal funds; while some executives have praised his maneuver as important economic development, others have sternly criticized the plan as a taxpayer-subsidized boondoggle. It remains the Perot Group's most visible—and speculative—project.

As time passed, it became plain that Perot was without an engrossing job. His separation agreement with GM required that he stay out of the computer business for three years. He could fume, but he was stuck in the water. He dabbled in rescue efforts for hostages, encouraged by the Joint Chiefs of Staff, the National Security Council, and a marine lieutenant colonel serving as an aide in the White House. He gave Oliver North $500,000 to ransom Brigadier General James Dozier, who had been kidnapped by Italy's Red Brigade. The money was returned after Dozier was freed by commandos. He helped provide medical care for soldiers wounded in Panama and Saudi Arabia, but somehow, as he passed his sixtieth birthday, he heard the ticking of a clock.

"He never changed," says Margot, "but he was . . . a little sad that he couldn't change things. That he couldn't solve [whatever problem came along, whether nuclear threat, terrorism, or deficit financing]. He always feels that he can solve the [world's] problem."

The "problems" have grown geometrically since Perot was a child growing up in an America where "anything was possible." Now, as Margot says, Solomon in all his wisdom can't solve our problems. The only person capable is Ross. It will, however, be at some sacrifice. "You know, we did look forward— I did—to this time in our lives when the children were grown and when we could just enjoy each other. Sit out in the boat—we have a small boat we keep at the lake—the two of us; he tinkers with the engine and I read mysteries. Fix a little breakfast in the morning. You're a thousand miles from anything."

But, she says, everything spun out of control. Instead of going to "nice places and forgetting about all the problems," instead of spending the night tinkering with the engine, Ross will have to tinker with the nation. "I think that people have to be told that, with enough effort, these problems can be solved."

Then came his appearance on the Larry King show and he was back showing his teeth, ready to solve the problem, running for president as an independent candidate, appealing to all those bewildered and alienated voters who were no longer inclined to trust the incumbent, George Bush, nor able to surrender to the Democratic challenger, Arkansas governor Bill Clinton. Only Ross Perot's outlaw style made them swoon.

In the wake of all that, when the five-dollar donations started pouring in and the volunteers lined up to handle the phones and ad-hoc committees sprang up like pollen, Perot hired a press-relations specialist, James Squires, and Tom Luce was back on board, running the campaign that had yet to officially exist. The machinery seemed to fall into place as headquarters opened, bumper stickers appeared, and Perot began to use unconventional means toward a conventional end. He appeared at a campaign rally in Orlando, Florida, which was transmitted by satellite to Ohio, Alabama, Kansas, Wyoming, and Idaho. He bypassed the usual vetting media process and appeared on talk shows, and his folksy, ordinary style of speech ("When something's wrong with the car, I'll be under the hood fixing it") seemed to dissipate the known fact that he was a billionaire. His commonsense approach to abortion (for it, but reluctantly), education (the only thing he would raise taxes for), the debt ("like the crazy aunt tucked away in the room upstairs nobody talks about"), taxing the wealthy ("Makes no sense for me to pay less of a percentage of my income than other people"), and aid to Russia to help them past their economic crisis ("the most cost-effective thing you can do"), rang true in a season of sour, false notes. He promised a coalition government, using the best minds of both parties. He said he would "get a shovel and clean out the barn."

Given the sparkling memory of his childhood and the luster of his married life, it was inevitable that he would give a lofty place to "family values" in his ragged platform. It was everybody's plank in 1992, but in Perot's case it didn't sound tinny.

The media hounded him for "positions" on issues, but he insisted he wasn't ready, and he went off to "think" in May, which caused consternation among the journalists. One was supposed to have positions tripping off one's lips, not lurking under layers of reflection. The hectoring of the press worked to his advantage, however. And his less-than-frantic urge to appease the media was a further comfort to a public annoyed to the breaking point with badgering reporters.

Opinions about him were wildly conflicting. He was either a heroic Paul Bunyon or an alarming merchant Attila the Hun. But, as Margot said, once he put his head down and got into it, he was a charging bull. He even broke the crust on his hard public personality and gave sweet interviews to the likes of Barbara Walters and a handful of reporters.

Of course, the decision to seek the presidency was not as sudden or whimsical as Perot would have you believe. When Perot and Meyerson discussed a race for the White House in February 1992, among the sensitive issues discussed was that of exclusionary clubs.

"I said to him, 'Ross, I know you belong to country clubs which exclude Jews and blacks—and as long as you're a private citizen you've got a right to do anything you want,'" Meyerson recalls. "'But when you're running for president you can't do that.' And he answered, 'I can't believe it'll be a problem to anybody, but if it is, I'll resign.'

"'Cause that's the way he is," Meyerson went on. "See, I'm Jewish, and I never raised Cain with him about it because I really didn't care. I think if you're in Dallas, Texas, it's not as big a thing as it would be if you're in New York." Nevertheless, when Perot's membership in restricted clubs became an issue (before the media got hold of it, in fact), Perot promptly quit.

In May, to avoid any potential conflict of interest, Perot also resigned as chairman and CEO of the Perot Group, turning control over to Meyerson.

Meyerson is sitting in the soft chair of a penthouse suite, thinking of the blend and break between Dallas and New York, thinking of the man who was so hardheaded that he wouldn't resign from a segregated club until pushed to the brink, until he risked losing something he cared about even more than his own stubborn pride. Then Meyerson says of Perot, "I think people underestimate Ross. They think he's naïve. They think he's a bumpkin. He looks like a shoe salesman. When he gets in the big leagues, what happens when he has to deal with Congress, what happens when he has to sit across from Mitterrand? I think people way underestimate Ross. He's one of the fastest studies I've ever seen. He won't make that mistake again."

There is the problem of a frisky nature and flinty temper. Perot will not suffer fools gladly; he could erupt at the press. It occurs to Meyerson that he is speaking, perhaps, of the next president of the United States. It is a thought that catches his imagination, draws lines across his forehead, and makes him wide-eyed with the implications. It is no longer a computer company after new business, it is no longer a hotspur boss off on a hare-brained adventure—it is the fate of the earth, it is posterity. Meyerson speaks thoughtfully: "But then, if he does blow up, well, maybe he shouldn't be president after all. You know, come to think of it, it's a pretty fair test."

Appendix:

November 2, 1991

When Ross Perot was recently asked to provide material that he felt accurately reflected his positions and views, he submitted the following speech, delivered to the Symposium for Better Government on November 2, 1991.

Through the happy accident of birth, we live in the greatest nation in the history of man. A strong, tough, resolute people created this country. The pioneers' creed sums the whole story up: "The cowards never started, the weak died on the way, and only the strong survived." These are the kinds of people who created our country. Read about the framers of the Constitution. Read about the signers of the Declaration. It's like you've just read about the people leading the revolution in Eastern Europe. Your mind will immediately go to Walesa, the shipyard worker in Poland who again and again and again risked his life against Russia. Now, you're wondering what the odds are you can make a difference. If you looked at Walesa's situation a few years ago you'd say, "Now, there's a guy that doesn't understand his problem," right? He made a difference because he was willing to put his life on the line for what he believed in. They didn't have any sound bites. They didn't have any handlers. They didn't have any image-makers. But they had strong beliefs, and that's what our country cries for today. They lived Patrick Henry's words.

Read the new book on George Washington, and your mind will immediately go to all these Democrats who say, "I don't think I want to run this time." Washington didn't want to run, but he ran because his nation needed him. These are the types of people we need in our country, and this has been our heritage. While you are here today, if the powerbrokers in Washington with their briefcases filled with money, their blow-dried hair, and their thousand-dollar suits took a minute to look down on this meeting, they would look on us with just total disdain and think how silly it is for ordinary people like you and me to think we could make a difference. They would say, "Who do you think you are anyhow? Why are you wasting your time? Don't you know we're just going to roll over you like Sherman tanks with all these hundreds of millions of dollars of special-interest money and television time in the next campaign? Don't you know how the political game is played?"

Well, like Walesa and other great people in our history, you're determined to change all that. Anybody who understood the problem would not have signed the Declaration of Independence. Anybody that had any sense at all would not have decided to fight against Great Britain in the Revolution. Now, that's a real kamikaze trip. But our people did, and they gave us this great country. So I needle you a little bit about the people who now have this thing under total control—not to discourage you, but to stir you up.

The last question that they'd ask is, "Who are these people anyhow?" I'd like to answer that question. I'd like to suggest that they read the Constitution. These are the people who own this country. If there are 250 million of us, you and I each own 1/250-millionth of this country. Now, most of us have forgotten it. Believe it or not, we own all those airplanes we see these guys flying around in. They're ours: not theirs. If you want to have a real thrill, try to borrow one to go to the dentist. The point is, never forget everybody up there works for you, and under our system of government, not only do they work for you, but they are your servants.

Well, at this point we'll have to conclude, I think, that the train has really gotten off the track in terms of who seems to be working for who, because you're working five months a year just paying taxes for them. We have a government turned upside down where the people running it act and live at your expense like royalty, and many of you are working two jobs just to stay even. That's not what the Constitution means. If you ever feel like you're all alone, here's the cover of *Time* magazine with George Washington with a tear in his eye. It says, "Is government dead?" Well, if it's not, it's in intensive care. You take your choice.

The point is most folks are taking the bus, and we've got all these leaders flitting around the country. I don't know why Dan Quayle needs to take my airplane, burn up tens of thousands of dollars worth of fuel to go play golf. There's probably somebody here that can explain that to me. Do you follow me? You know, all these congressmen, as soon as Congress is out, go get an Air Force plane and fly all over the world on junkets and don't accomplish a thing. But, see, these trips are paid for right out of our hides, and these are things that are just dramatic proof, I suggest to you, that we've got the world turned upside down. I think I speak for everyone in this audience when I say we really love this country. In an audience this size, there are people who have left parts of their bodies on the battlefield. There are widows of people who died in action. There are family members who lost sons or daughters. Those are the ultimate expressions of love for your country. We love the principles that this country was founded on, and we don't like to see these great principles violated.

My speech today I've dedicated to millions of American citizens who feel like we do but don't ever get to talk to an audience of several thousand people, don't get to speak on national television, and are becoming disillusioned and cynical. That's the worst thing that can happen. What if our founders had given up? They didn't give up, and yet millions of us have. It's been pointed out that only slightly over 36 percent voted in the last election. They just signed off. We can't let that happen because it's our country, and we can't abdicate the responsibilities of ownership.

After the election people like us go back to work. We have to go back to work because we're going to work five months just to pay our taxes. Most of us are not organized into special-interest groups. We don't have somebody roaming the halls of Congress for us all day every day with a satchel full of money. More and more we understand that while we are the voters and we are the people, we do not have an effective voice. The people that I am committed to and I'm sure you are committed to are the people who work hard, who play by the rules, who operate in the center of the field of ethical behavior. They've lived their lives by what's right and wrong; not what's legal and illegal. They obey the law. They rear good children. They're patriots.

I spoke to audiences of 18,000 people when we had the buildup for the Persian Gulf. Most of these were business executives. I found eight people in my audiences of 18,000 that had sons or daughters in the Middle East. I got their concurrence that it's the people who work for them whose sons and daughters had their lives on the line for all of us. I proposed that we have a war tax before we go into this so that all of us had skin in the game, and anybody who didn't want to pay it could go into battle because those are the guys who pay no taxes. I didn't get much interest on that. People asked me why I did that: I wanted to see how deep this commitment was. We looked on this as a Super Bowl.

Believe me, war is not a Super Bowl. If I had more time, we could spend a lot of time on that. War is not bombs going down air shafts. War is great young people getting killed, getting pieces of their bodies blown away. War is the last resort, and if and when we do go to war, we must commit the nation and then commit the troops. Never again should we get into a Vietnam situation where we send men and women off to fight and die.

Well, God bless Congress. They finally voted a resolution on this one. They didn't want to, but they did. They wanted to run, duck, and hide. You don't run, duck, and hide and send your son out and my son out to die. I'd a whole lot rather vote to go to war than go to war, wouldn't you? I mean, that's pretty simple. Then, just to show how corrupt our system is, first off the reason we had to do this is because we told Saddam Hussein he could take the northern part of Kuwait and then got upset when he took the whole thing. We had to send the sons and daughters of working people off to fix that.

When it was all over and everybody got all the publicity, I said, "Where is Sergeant York? Where are the battlefield heroes? Why are there no pictures of the wounded?" Isn't it bizarre that the only heroes from this war are generals and politicians? Think about it. Were there battlefield heroes? You bet there were. How do I know? I know their widows. I know the parents who are still heartbroken, and I know the wounded whose lives will never be the same. We had our battlefield heroes. In any properly run government, they would have been the heroes in our war as they have always before. In any properly run government, a cross-section of America would have been on the battlefield. FDR's sons flew missions in World War II. Two members of Congress had sons on the battlefield in the Persian Gulf conflict.

This is a country that stands squarely on the broad shoulders of ordinary people. That's the way it was intended to be. You are the steel and concrete that holds our country together. Never forget it. You are givers in a greedy world filled with takers. You are very special people—the people who do the honest work in our country. De Tocqueville was talking about you when he concluded that America is great because her people are good. Then he went on to say, "If the American people ever cease being good, America will cease being great." Don't turn off. Don't become disillusioned or cynical, because you are the greatness of America. You say, "Well,

I'm just an ordinary person." We don't have a prayer without you, and I'll explain why in a minute. You're paying the bills for everything we do. You're paying the bills for our mistakes. You're the majority of the electorate. Let's look at where our great nation is. First off, let me just say this: It's a situation where nobody's taken out the trash here at home for a long time and nobody's cleaned out the barn. Now, on any given day, we'll be out there somewhere trying to solve somebody else's problems, but we've forgotten something very, very basic. Right now in a world of sound bites, we like to posture and gloat like a Saturday-night wrestler after the event that we are the only superpower left, and we love to refer to ourselves as the only superpower. Give me a break! You can't be a superpower unless you're rich.

Let's bring it down on a personal level. Let's assume there's a great person in your community who's always been very generous and very helpful, like our country's been. Suddenly he's just gone broke. Can he give to the United Way anymore? Can he give to the Salvation Army? Can he help anybody? No, he needs help. We must be economically strong if we are going to continue to be the kind of nation we want to be. It takes money to clean out the barn and take out the trash right here, so we have got to stop sleepwalking about our financial condition. We're the largest debtor nation. We have a debt of $3.5 trillion we admit to and another $6 trillion that's kind of like a crazy aunt we keep in the basement. All the neighbors know she's there, but nobody talks much about it. If we're not financially strong, we cannot solve our problems at home. We cannot defend ourselves and others throughout the world. If we want to help other people in other nations in need, we must have money. That means we've got to get our country back on a sound financial footing.

There are people in this audience who fought in World War II. Let's assume I'd come here in 1950 and said, "During our lifetime, Germany and Japan will be the world's two economic superpowers." You guys would have thrown me out. It would never happen. They were in ashes. Mr. Honda was wandering around the streets of Japan, a high-school graduate, looking for scrap iron to make a motor scooter. He's come a long way, baby. Toyota was bankrupt in 1951. The number-three car maker in the world. They've come a long way, and I could go on and on. Well, let's take a look at these. What do they have in common? Their countries and economies were destroyed at the end of World War II. They were in ashes. Out of adversity comes strength. That's as old as civilization, as old as human nature. But we did a service for them that they would never have figured out how to do on their own. We forced new constitutions on them in 1945. Talk to the leading Japanese businessmen and they will be forever grateful to General MacArthur for that constitution.

We're losing entire industries to international competitors. I know and am a friend of the man who holds the basic patents on the integrated circuit, who is still alive. Today, nineteen out of twenty integrated circuits used in our great country come from Japan. We used to be the country that did things no one could do. We gave the world the electric light. We taught the world to fly and on and on. Nobody could build the Panama Canal. We went down there and built it. Now we create these things and lose them because those governments have an intelligent relationship between government and business and ours is adversarial. The business leaders in the country have not been good stewards. Their job is to create and protect jobs in America—not in Mexico.

Let's look at what they did during the '80s. The

junk bonds that destroyed jobs, destroyed companies, and created damage to savings and loans and banks and financial institutions in the hundreds of billions of dollars. You say, "Well, who's going to pay for that?" Go home tonight and look in the mirror. Pretty soon you're going to say, "Ross, if I've got to pay for all this, I'd better have a good job." You bet you'd better have a good job, and that leads me right back to where I started. You are the job base, and our number one challenge in this country is to keep that job base intact and expanding. We have a few people, our business leaders, who can create jobs and millions of fine, wonderful people who are more than happy to work at a job and do a good job. But the words of a meat packer in an Iowa meat-packing plant that closed, an older man, never taken anything from anybody and was forced to go on welfare, summed it all up. He said, "I did not quit my job. My job quit me." That's the business leaders' responsibility to make sure that doesn't happen, and it's government's responsibility to make sure in international competition that American industry has a fair chance.

I'd give anything if the president would come home to Washington, get a who's who of corporate America into his offices in small numbers, and say,

"Okay, guys, starting tomorrow, we have got to make the words 'made in the USA' the world's standard for excellence once again. I want you guys who run these companies to get out of the country clubs, get off the golf course, get out of your jets, and get down there on the factory floors seven days a week and don't come out until it's done! First thing tomorrow morning, I want you to get rid of your golden parachutes and all this obscene stuff you've got and let all the troops down on the factory floor know that sacrifice starts at the top. That'll be a start. If you don't get rid of all of that, I'm going to send a bill to Congress to tax it at 100 percent, and that will be the most popular law that ever went through the Congress."

All this junk bond stuff, cut it out! Stop diddling. Our economy is like a tired old racehorse that was a great old racehorce but now has arthritis in his legs. We shod it up for 1988. You go back to 1984, the president of the United States was told, "Fix the savings and loan problem now and it's a $20 billion problem." They waited until after the election, and it became a $200 billion problem. Nobody knows what it is now. It's somewhere out there between $200 and $500 billion. That's such a big amount of money, nobody can relate to it.

But the facts are, we have got to cut all that goofy stuff out and get back to basics. There was my two-year experience with General Motors. That was interesting. The fallout, believe me, was not on the factory floor. The people on the factory floor were the salt of the earth. They are the people who were farming and ranching when I was a boy who are now working inside. These are the folks who are just the salt of the earth. I used to spend time in the factories. Nobody ever came around to me whining for more pay, more benefits, more this for me. They were concerned about the quality of the car to protect their job. That's it! They don't have a voice in it, so when you get right down to it, it's the guys at the top calling the plays that determine the quality of the product coming out at the end. Forty-two percent of your income is now going to pay taxes. Our government consumes 25 percent, or one-fourth, of our gross national product. My question is, do you think you're getting your money's worth? Isn't that sad? You bought a front-row seat in the box, and you're seeing a fourth-rate vaudeville show from the balcony.

I don't understand a government where the White House and the Congress spend all their time throwing rocks at one another, and we the people are paying for that rock-throwing contest and don't get the results. By any candid observation, the American people are the nicest people in the world, they're the most passionate people in the world, but they're the most stupid people in the world. Let me just give you an example. Last year, here goes what I call the Washington shell game. First we have, "Watch my lips. No new taxes." Like rabbits we ran down to vote for that. It worked. Use whatever works when you're running. Then we had to raise taxes. Then we went through all the posturing and the blowhard and what have you, and they passed a total of a $166.5 billion in new taxes and we the people were told, "That'll take care of it." They didn't tell us at the same time they authorized new expenditures of $304 billion, or $1.83 of new expenses for every dollar they collected. Now, there's a shell game for you.

If I'm going to pick your pocket, I don't think I would give myself a raise and build myself a new gymnasium with that money, but they did. We just kind of sit here like trained rabbits or like Lawrence Welk, "Wunnerful, wunnerful, wunnerful," and send them on back up there. I don't blame them for robbing the bank in broad daylight as long as we keep patting them on the back and sending them back up there. Neither Congress nor the White House pointed out all this new spending.

We were told before the taxing summit and budget summit that our 1991 deficit would be only $63.1 billion. By the next April, they gave us a new forecast of $318 billion, and that's a $255 billion mistake. I say, who's keeping books here? Folks, nobody's keeping books up there.

. If you've ever been around a company going bankrupt, they stop keeping books at a certain point in time because it's so unpleasant to look at the numbers. They also told us that if we agreed to all these taxes, the deficit over five years would only be in the $90 billion range. A few months later, we were told it would be $1 trillion. That's a $900 billion mistake. Well, they're now forecasting just next year's deficit to be $348 billion. That's the Office of Management and Budget. They've got a set of books over there. Now let's go over to Congress. They've got a different set of books. They say it will not be $384 billion, but $425 billion. It's your money, so what difference does it make? You're so good-natured about sending it, what difference does it make? That's a $77 billion difference. See, a billion dollars is so big, nobody can figure out what it is. It's pretty simple. We can't grasp a number of this magnitude but let me try to bring it home and say, "Okay, we're going to pay up last year's deficit, the one that just ended." Let's confiscate the *Forbes* 400 wealth. Sorry, we didn't get enough. "You mean we took all the rich people's money and we can't pay one year's deficit?" No. Well, let's sell General Motors and Exxon and put the money in the U.S. Treasury. That won't do it either. Okay, let's really get dramatic and confiscate all the profits for one year from the *Fortune* 500 companies and give that to the U.S. Treasury. That won't get half of it. This helps you see how big it is. Isn't there somewhere we could get this much money? Oh, yeah, I can think of one place. If I could get Japan to give us their largest bank and if I could sell it to the Arabs, then I would have enough to pay one year's deficit. That shows you how big it is and how serious the problem is. I'm sure you're saying, "Well, wait a minute, Ross. If the biggest bank in the world is in Japan, what ever happened to the biggest bank—we used to have all the biggest banks." In the language of the street, here's what happened. They made better products than we did. We bought their products with what used to be our money. They now have what used to be our money in their banks. What used to be our money earns interest twenty-four hours a day, seven days a week. You know, money in the bank earns interest on holidays. A working guy can't work night and day, he can't work Christmas Day and what have you. He needs Sunday off. Money never stops. We've got their products, whose value deteriorates the day we start buying them, in our garages and in our living rooms. Who's winning and who's losing? It's pretty simple. Pretty simple. It's back to who's making the best products. If you want the biggest banks in the world, make the best products here. Can we? Absolutely! Are we going to? I don't know, but I know we have to.

We can go through two cycles. We've got two choices at this point. I'm going to ask for an unnatural act in a free society. I'm going to ask for us to look at our situation. We're like alcoholics now who still think we're social drinkers. We're still going through denial. We've got to look in the mirror and say, "You know, we're drinking too much and we'd better quit." But while our tax base is still relatively intact, while our people are still at work, while we still have a manageable situation, we had better go into overdrive to fix these things to keep this great economic engine going and to rebuild it and not go into a serious drought. It's been a long time since it rained as far as Detroit is concerned. I'll tell you that right now. We have our work cut out for us.

Our government makes some interesting excuses for the numbers being this far off. The Office of Management and Budget blames the Treasury Department. I'm underwhelmed. It's not as though the Treasury Department is in Russia. Both of those belong to the president of the United States, and if they can't keep books in sync with one another, it's his job to straighten them out. How can things get this far out of control? In our country we have 332 incompatible accounting systems. We have our accounting designed so that we don't know what's going on. On a down-to-earth level, we've got 319 different payroll systems so we can't even balance the payroll. We have an antiquated IRS system that fails to collect billions of dollars each year in taxes, just to mention a few. And last year, the comptroller of the currency, chosen by the president of the United States, said that we are squandering and wasting $180 billion through waste, fraud, mismanagement, and abuse. That's not a bad pocket to start in right there.

I'm going to help you put these in perspective. The federal debt for the entire ten-year period of the 1940s when we fought World War II—now go back to when you guys were on the battlefield—did not exceed $31.7 billion. That's less than one-tenth of this year's deficit. World War II cost $288 billion, and we paid for it as we went and that's the way you ought to pay your bills. Today, interest payments on the federal debt take 58 cents out of every personal income tax dollar you send to Uncle Sam. I'm hoping to make you uncomfortable with that. If we don't change something and we keep on the present trends, 102 cents out of every income tax dollar will go to pay interest on the debt. That doesn't pay the debt.

In this environment, the Senate gave itself the 23 percent raise. Do you know any working people who got a 23 percent raise? Isn't it weird? See, you're the boss. They work for you. You didn't get a raise. They gave themselves a 23 percent raise and we just kind of grin like, "Well, you know, boys will be boys." There's no accountability. They now have over 20,000 people on their staffs, and I can promise you if you ever call up there as just an ordinary citizen, in most cases you'll be treated rudely. That's sad. I had so many letters saying that, I finally just wandered around the halls the other day unannounced and got a generous dose of it myself. These young people out there on the front desk don't know who I am. I don't look like much. They just acted like some Martian had come in, and I included the Texas delegation in some of these visits!

Now, contrast that to when I was a midshipman at the Naval Academy. My mother, God bless her, had never gotten to go anywhere. She finally saved enough money so she could see the academy. We went to Washington. We wanted to see the Capitol. We went into the Capitol. We thought it would be nice to meet our congressman. To say we were nobody would be an overstatement. We walked into the office of the majority leader of the Senate, Lyndon Johnson, and announced that we were from Texas and we'd like to see the senator. We were immediately ushered into his office and talked with him for fifteen minutes. Quite a change. Try that today. Even if you went to a $1,000-a-plate dinner, try that today. Accountability and contact with people has gotten lost.

In 1993, the interest alone on the debt will be $320 billion a year. Let me put that in perspective for you. Hold on to your seat. In the first 155 years of our government's existence, we did not spend that much money to operate the government of the United States. But next year we'll have a deficit that exceeds that amount—excuse me, an interest on the deficit. This is just interest. When I talk about interest, remember interest doesn't buy anything. It doesn't buy a thing. It's just paying down on something you've already got.

We can't comprehend a trillion dollars. Let me try two ways to get it over to you. Do you know how long it would take to count to a trillion if you counted one number a second? It would take 31,700 years. But you say, "Wait a minute, Ross. We've got over $4 trillion next year." That's right. That's over 120,000 years just to count it. Let me give it to you another way. What if we just stacked thousand-dollar bills one on top of the other right here, packed them tight? You'd have a stack sixty-three miles into space of thousand-dollar bills. To help you understand a billion, you'd have a stack three hundred feet high. Three hundred feet high is a billion, so we're talking big bucks here when we talk a trillion. Until the average citizen gets upset, this three-act comedy we've got going on up there will continue.

Let me tell you what a trillion would have bought for every citizen. For everybody in the state of Kansas, Missouri, Nebraska, Oklahoma, and Iowa, we could have bought and paid cash for a $100,000 house and put a $10,000 car in

every garage and built 250 $10 million libraries
in those states and built 250 $10 million hospit-
als in those states and built 500 $10 million schools
in those states and with the interest on what's left
over, pay 10,000 nurses and teachers and give a
$5,000-a-year bonus to every family in those states.
That's what $1 trillion working hard here at home
would buy. But we're $4 trillion down. So instead of
just those five states that I mentioned, with $4 tril-
lion we can buy all of those things for everybody in
all of the New England and Middle Atlantic states
—eleven of them, our most populous states. That's
how much money we've thrown out the window.

We've got work to do. With this much expendi-
ture, we ought to have utopia. Can you agree on
that? All right, let's look at the scoreboard. We're
getting ready to clean out the barn now. We're the
largest debtor nation in the history of man. We're
the most violent, crime-ridden nation in the industrialized world. Isn't it weird for those of you who
grew up in the Depression that you didn't have to
lock the doors when everybody was broke? The
most violent, crime-ridden nation in the industrialized world! We rank at the bottom of the industrialized world in terms of academic achievement. We
have the largest number of functional illiterates in

the industrialized world in our workforce. You and I can remember, those who are my age, when our public school system was the envy of the world. We've got to fix that. I went around the world, took a year on destroyers with sailors who grew up in the Depression. I was the youngest officer. I got aboard the night we left, so I was the youngest officer when we got back, so I got all the dirty jobs. One of them was shore patrol everywhere. If you said, "Ross, did those guys miss anything?" I'd say, "No, I think they tried it all." Then if you had said, "But did they try drugs?" I'd have said, "Oh, no. Sailors don't try drugs. Everybody knows that stuff will kill you." You'd say, "Were there drugs around?" There were drugs everywhere. Today we're 5 percent of the world's population. We use 50 percent of the world's cocaine. We've got to fix this. Talk is cheap. Holding a two-day educational summit in Williamsburg, Virginia, folks, is a waste of time. Reading to school children on television for political purposes is a waste of time. That is not the highest and best use of our skill. Interestingly enough, we're the most litigious society in the industrialized world. We've got 5 percent of the world's population, two-thirds of the world's lawyers, and the average citizen can't afford to hire one. Think about it. We've got the world's most expensive health-care system but rank sixteenth place in life expectancy in the world and twenty-third place in infant mortality. Something's wrong. Our money is not being spent intelligently, is the point I'm trying to make, and perhaps I made it too well.

I get a lot of mail from ordinary people. I have friends remind me all the time of how lucky I've been. There was a man at General Motors when I was there who was so bright as a young man, he was accepted at MIT. Just coming out of World War II, he couldn't afford to go. Then he was accepted at West Point and failed the eye exam. He spent his life on the factory floor. The difference between him and myself is that I passed the eye exam to the Naval Academy and got to go to college. But this country is filled with wonderful bright people who didn't get that break.

I want you to listen to this letter. I'm going to read short excerpts from it. Ask yourself, "Is this a college professor or who is it that's writing to Perot?" Here it is, and this is the core of what I want to say to you today, and these are not my words. "Democracy is like passion. You can't fake it. It's like love, courage, or even common sense. If it doesn't come from us, we don't have it. Yet, where is the way, the means, for something to come from us and come in a way that makes a difference? We now have a government that comes almost entirely at us. We are told what we should want, what we should fear, what we should believe in, who to vote for and even what we should look like. We the people have become some vast, second-guessed, lowest common denominator. In effect, we are the market. We are the rabbits that they're advertising to. Our political process comes at us with all of the honesty and relevance of a Coca-Cola commercial. Indeed, we choose our representatives like we choose our soda pop, and with equal similarity, once we've chosen them, all we get is gas.

"Sometimes frustration rises until people feel like throwing the rascals out. I wish it were that easy. This is not really an answer. The rascals are like scum on the surface of a pond with no inlet or outlet. It rises to the top because the water is stagnant. You can skim all you want, but new scum will form. The answer is to get the water moving—and that's us! We need something fresh and strong and consistent coming from us in a way that can no longer be ignored. But that would take a change in us because we sit back with the attitude of let the pros do it, and, believe me, they are doing it to us."

As I sum this up, I'd like for you to think of the dreams you had as a child. Think of the sacrifices your parents made for you. Think of the signers of the Declaration of Independence, and ask yourself, "Am I going to be another one of these characters who just wants to put his image on the front page or am I willing to put it on the line to clean this mess up for my children?" If you want to know why I'm here, I'm really concerned about the world my children and grandchildren will live in. I feel rotten that I am spending their money. I feel I have a tremendous obligation as a private citizen while I'm here to try to pay that debt off and give them the opportunities that all of us had throughout our lives.

Okay, it's going to take action and not talk. In all fairness to our elected officials—they are generally good people—they are not the problem. Our system of government is the problem. If we threw them all out, put a new crop in, if we went up there, within twelve months, having these guys running around tickling you behind the ear telling you how great you are and handing you money, we'd be just like they are. You've got to change the system! Keep in mind our Constitution predates the industrial revolution. Our founders did not know about electricity, the train, telephones, radios, television, automobiles, airplanes, rockets, nuclear weapons, satellites, or space exploration. There's a lot they didn't know about. It would be interesting to see what kind of document they'd draft today. Just keeping it frozen in time won't hack it. We need to follow Churchill's words. The thing the staff around Churchill would tell you he said most frequently all during World War II is, "Action this day!" Now, that'll cause people to fall over and faint in Washington, but you don't get anything done until you take action.

What can we do? Let me just run through a short list and I'll button it up. Here are just a few simple ideas. You'll have better ones than I have. Let's take away the right of Congress to raise taxes because they're acting irresponsibly. If they want to raise taxes, put it on the ballot, and if you think it's worthwhile we'll do it. Let's cut out the deficit spending—just right now, cut it. Expenditures cannot exceed revenues. When you start down this path, don't blink. You'd better have the Orkin man with you. You're going to have to eliminate the tricks, the loopholes, and the improper accounting procedures, but that can be done if you stay focused.

Give the president a line-item veto on the budget. Three reasons. Number one, I'd like him to quit whining about not having it. Second, I'd like to see what he does with it, and, thirdly, if we get real lucky, he'll cut out a lot of pork barrel.

Absolutely get the Orkin man and get rid of all the PACs. That's a curse on our country. You've got to get rid of them. The maximum contribution $1,000, no exceptions. Anything else is criminal, both to the guy running for office and the guy that gave it to him.

Cut the time for an election campaign to five months. Who do you think owns the airwaves in this country? You do. Who do you think gives the right to all these television stations to broadcast? You do. Do you realize that a well-run television station can bring 50 percent of its revenues down to profits? You've been giving these airwaves away too cheap, folks. You ought to get some kind of fee from that, but you don't. You just give it to them. Now, then, in this five-month election cycle, let's go to these fellows that are getting rich at our expense and say, "We want free television time and it would be divided equally among the candidates." They'd no longer have to sell their souls to the devil. Good people with no money have to sell their souls to get the TV time to run, and that's rotten. Let's say you run into some hard-nosed guy who says, "I'm not going to give you time." You say, "Fine. Next time your permit comes up, we'll give it to someone else." He'll follow you around the block to give you the time with the kind of money he's making!

Require every member of Congress to turn in their excess campaign funds to the U.S. Treasury—now! They'd say, "Wait a minute, Ross. I've been around here twenty years. Aren't you going to grandfather me?" No, I want your money first, sucker, because you've got the big pile.

We've got congressmen that have $15 million in their war chest, and we have a system of government that they created and we sat here with our thumbs in our mouths where they can take it with them when they retire. Did you ever hear of anything like that anywhere else? Maybe in the drug business, but nowhere else.

Only in America would you hold elections on Tuesday. A working guy's got to go to work. If he's first shift, he goes to work 8:30 to 5:30. That's an hour and a half in the morning and an hour and a half at night. Let's have elections on the weekends. Why not have it Saturday and Sunday? And let's make it a criminal offense to release any information from East Coast polls before the Hawaii polling booths are closed.

Now, if you had these kinds of problems in your company, you'd go down there and seize financial control. We just did that. We grabbed the taxes. I would also, as a matter of principle, make sure that we get rid of all these strange freebies that float around. For example, free haircuts, free parking, free gymnasiums—how many of you have a free gymnasium? It's interesting that the guys who work for you have one. You paid for it. They built one with that tax increase that was supposed to pay down the deficit. They built a new one. Anybody ever get free prescription drugs when you want them? Anybody get a free ambulance ride? Anybody get free airport parking?

I also recommend we eliminate all government-provided transportation on government jets, except one exception—Air Force One, and I'd put it on the question list. You say, "Why are you being so hard?" I want to capture their minds and hearts. I want to let them know that we the people run this country and not those fellows up there that are in the halls every day tickling them behind the ear. That means every member of Congress goes commercial. He goes out there, he gets in line, he gets his baggage lost, he eats a bad meal, and he just kind of gets used to the way we live. It might influence how they run the airlines. One other thing we'd do is sell all those airplanes and use the money to pay down the debt. Most important here is the symbolism, though. You've got to capture people's minds and hearts and let them know you're serious.

If Congress wants a raise—we took care of taxes —we'd say, "Okay, fellows, you want a raise? From now on, put it on the ballot. If we think you're doing a good job, we'll give you one." They'll tear their hair.

Now, then, first thing in the morning and before the sun sets, all these laws you've passed on civil rights, disabilities, equal opportunity, occupational safety, and fair labor standards for us and exempted yourselves from, drop that yoke right around your shoulders tomorrow and play by the same rules as us.

We just figured out last night that you boys set up a retirement fund for yourselves that pays two to three times as much as a normal retirement fund pays for us, your bosses. Cut it back to what we get. Don't even think about it. There's one other thing. We just figured out that ninety-three members of the House and Senate are eligible for lifetime pension benefits—these are individual—exceeding $2 million apiece. Get real! Come down to earth.

We're spending $2.3 billion a year just to support Congress and its agencies. Slash the cost and improve the service. Pass laws—and this is very dear to my heart—that no former federal official elected or appointed can serve as a lobbyist for five years after they leave office.

Okay, now watch my lips on this one—and nobody can lobby for a foreign country for at least ten years. And closest to my heart of all is that a former president cannot lobby for anybody, foreign or domestic, ever. I would want strong criminal penalties there because I am sick and tired of former presidents going to Japan and making two twenty-minute speeches and getting a $2 million payday. That just breaks my heart.

We would dramatically reduce the White House staff and all the departments of government. I'm talking Agriculture, all these. We've just got thousands of people out there massaging the situation. But remember this—headquarters staffs accomplish very little. It's the soldiers in the field who are important. All that overhead is a waste of money.

These are just a few ideas. You'll have better

ideas. We've got to start acting like owners. We've got to change the system and put it back in your control. Here's just one question as I close my speech. Is this another Williamsburg summit? Is this another place where we're going to posture and talk and then leave and go whine and suck our thumbs? Or are we going to strap it on and go out and do it? Now, that's the challenge—to do it! There's no question in my mind if you'll just go out and do it that we can remain a kind and gentle giant, a friend to all in need. We can be the type of country that we have wanted to be and want to be. But we must be economically strong and we must have our house in order and we must have our tax base in order and we must make the best products in the world to create that tax base.

If we do that, we will be able to do what I was taught before they wouldn't let you teach ethics in public schools. In the Depression we were forced to memorize a little poem. It says:

> Help the man who is down today,
>   Give him a lift in his sorrow.
>   Life has a very strange way.
> No one knows what may happen tomorrow.

Let's get started now. My personal goal—and I think it's a good goal for all of you—is to leave our children what our parents left us: a better world and a better country and a stronger country than they found; were they to use the phrase from one of the songs in the musical *The Sound of Music*, that our children when they're grown can "climb every mountain, ford every stream, and follow every rainbow" until they find their dream. God bless you. Good to be with you.

About the Author

KEN GROSS is a magazine writer and a former columnist for *New York Newsday*. A recipient of the Meyer Berger Award for journalism, he is the author of nine previous books of fiction and nonfiction. He lives in Brooklyn, New York, with his wife and son.

About the Type

This book was set in Electra, a typeface designed for
Linotype by W. A. Dwiggins, the renowned type designer
(1880–1956). Electra is a fluid typeface, avoiding the contrasts of thick and thin strokes that are prevalent in most
modern typefaces.